MAGNETIC MARKETING FOR LAWYERS

MAGNETIC MARKETING FOR LAWYERS

HOW TO ATTRACT A FLOOD OF NEW CLIENTS THAT **PAY, STAY,** AND **REFER**

DAN S. KENNEDY
AND RJON ROBINS

Advantage®

Published by Advantage, Charleston, South Carolina.
Member of Advantage Media Group.

Printed in the United States of America.

10 9 8 7 6 5 4 3 2 1

ISBN: 978-1-642252-65-1
LCCN: 2021901199

Contents

BUILDING YOUR MAGNETIC MARKETING SYSTEM

INTRODUCTION

Learn the Secrets of the Most Successful Lawyers Who Have Created a Flood of New Clients

You have finally found it!

The one place created for lawyers seeking to answer that common, nagging question:

"I am a great lawyer, so why aren't the best clients finding my law firm?"

All law firms, regardless of their practice area, face the same challenge—how to attract a steady stream of the right kinds of clients, with the right kinds of cases, predictably, reliably, and consistently, enough to produce steady (and growing) cash flow, warranting enough confidence to decline work from crazy clients with crappy cases just to make payroll next month.

If this doesn't resonate with you, chances are you aren't the owner of the law firm you work for. If you do own a law firm, then it probably does. And regardless of practice area, no matter the staff complement, and irrespective of past success, we want to congratulate you for being an entrepreneur.

Rest assured, while you hold this book in your hands, you are with other like-minded entrepreneurs—friends who know what it's like to sit in the seat where "the buck stops."

This book is 100 percent based upon real-world, direct-response, education-based law firm marketing strategies that have the power to magnetize your law firm, to attract the right kinds of clients who have the right kinds of cases. Each strategy you're soon to discover in the pages that follow has been proven by thousands of mostly solo and small law firm owners in a wide range of practice areas, practicing in large cities and small towns. They're men and women, all ages, all attitudes, all walks of life; some of them are right-handed, some left.

And remember, magnets both attract and repel! So equally important, these strategies and the step-by-step tactics we will share with you (including case studies) will also magnetize your law firm to protect you from the wrong kinds of clients and/or the right kinds of clients who just don't happen to have the right kinds of cases for your law firm.[1]

You have worked hard, created a solid reputation, and done great work with a long list of happy and appreciative clients. But you've discovered that being a great lawyer doesn't automatically mean a great lawyer's law firm becomes magnetic to prospective new clients.

You've likely long suspected it, so let us confirm it for you that the lawyers who are out there at bar functions bragging that their law firm gets all of their business by reputation and referral … either they're lying to you, or their law firm isn't serving nearly as many clients as it could be (a polite way to say they're broke). Or else those bragging lawyers are naive to the facts and there is a grown-up attending to the marketing of the law firm so that the children at the kiddies' table don't have to concern themselves with where the food comes from.

Being a great lawyer doesn't automatically mean your law firm becomes magnetic to prospective new clients.

1 Re: Case studies. We know you're a lawyer, so you may have an emotional need to see plenty of case studies. The ones you see in this book are only the tip of the iceberg, as we are limited by our publisher for page count. If you want to see plenty, plenty, plenty more, please visit MagneticMarketingForLawyers.com/CaseStudies.

You've tried marketing: you've spent serious money on ads that didn't work, direct mail that underdelivered, pay-per-click advertising that drained your bank account dry, and probably a host of other approaches, none of which delivered the results promised or expected.

Like most lawyers who own their firm, you sometimes feel confused and overwhelmed, getting hammered on all sides with "consultants" saying do one thing or another and feeling like you have to press harder to do more and more—just to get the same results. Or less.

We are here to help you—to mute all that noise and provide you with a set of practical and proven principles, not just theories, tactics, or the latest technology. We'll also be sharing the resources you'll need to magnetically attract clients who are ready, willing, and able to engage your firm to help them have a better future. And by that we mean a duplicatable machine for not only attracting clients but also converting leads into appointments, appointments into clients, and multiplying one client into two.

Marketing is an ever-changing world, as new media seems to pop up every day, but if you learn the principles that allow some of the most successful law firms in the country to become magnetically attractive to clients, you can make any media work, in any market, at any time regardless of what might be happening with "everyone else."

When you develop a system that feeds new clients to your firm on a daily basis, you will never again have to feel the anxiety of wondering when or where your next case will come from! In fact, you can finally know the answer to the question that haunts so many hundreds of thousands of struggling solo and small law firm owners:

"I am a great lawyer, so why aren't the best clients finding my law firm?"

THE THINKING BEHIND THIS BOOK

Before we get far into this book, let's address an elephant that may well be lurking in the room.

If you are a serious student of marketing, you may have read the original version of this book written by Dan Kennedy, or you may have heard of his Magnetic Marketing System and Toolkit. Over the past twenty-five years, with these resources, Dan has generated many tens of millions of dollars for himself and spawned billions in revenue for small businesses and entrepreneurs throughout the world, including plenty of lawyers.

Dan is a multimillionaire serial entrepreneur with past and present interests in diverse businesses. He is a strategic advisor, marketing consultant, and coach with a cadre of private high-end clients ranging from exceptionally ambitious entrepreneurs to the CEOs of companies as large as $1.5 billion. He's one of the most sought-after and highest-paid direct-response copywriters in the world, as well as a popular seminar leader and speaker who has shared the stage with Gene Simmons (KISS), Joan Rivers, Debbi Fields (Mrs. Fields Cookies), Jim McCann (1-800-FLOWERS.com), and Donald Trump before hundreds of thousands of entrepreneurs around the world.

Dan is a legend in the world of direct-response marketing and anyone out there advising, consulting, teaching, or benefiting from direct-response marketing principles today, if they have truly studied their craft, knows it all traces back to Dan, who himself acknowledges that the lineage extends much further back than himself and that he benefits from standing on the shoulders of many other marketing giants. Benjamin Franklin, by way of example, was a devoted student of business, an able practitioner of marketing, and became extravagantly wealthy before his Founding Father days—all by using many of the same timeless principles Dan has been employing to make more millionaires alive today than just about any other person on this planet.

And so, you may be wondering three things:

1. **Why write a book titled *Magnetic Marketing for Lawyers*?**
2. **Is this going to be just a mediocre, "search and replace" version of the original material, or does this book provide valuable, new, and unique insights that make it especially relevant for law firm marketing?**
3. **Why did Dan ask RJon to be his coauthor?**

If you have already studied Dan's original work, *Magnetic Marketing* (not just for lawyers), here in this new book you will discover a great deal of new material along with new ways to apply original material specifically to the marketing of a small law firm. We've collected and shared dozens of law firm–specific examples and case studies, and of course you will benefit from the unique perspective of Dan's coauthor, RJon Robins.

Yes, RJon is a licensed attorney, but what's probably much more relevant and important for you to know is that RJon is the founder and CEO of How to Manage a Small Law Firm—the largest and fastest-growing provider of outside "time-share" CEO, COO, and CFO services for solo and small law firms in the country. How to Manage a Small Law Firm manages more than four hundred of the fastest-growing and some of the most profitable solo and small law firms in the world.

But that doesn't answer the question "Why write a book, *Magnetic Marketing* for Lawyers?" Why wouldn't Dan just rest on his laurels?

Let's just say, if you have to ask that question, you don't know Dan. Several years ago Dan was thinking, "It would be really interesting to begin exploring all the ways my students have been adapting and applying the lessons I've shared over the past several decades to build so many multimillion-dollar businesses—especially in a few industries that are particularly well-known for their pathetically god-awful marketing!"

Right about that time is when RJon purchased his seat in Dan's world-famous ***Titanium Group***. This is an application-only, very high-end, and exclusive Mastermind group. To give you an idea, and to demonstrate the power of making yourself magnetic to your ideal clients, Titanium enjoys a two-year waiting list. To even be considered for "a seat at the table" in Titanium, candidates must complete a written application and demonstrate substantial financial means. (Just imagine what it would do for your life if your law firm had a steady enough flow of prospective new clients that you actually had to have a waiting list!)

Part of the selection criteria for securing and holding onto one of only fifteen seats includes the willingness and ability to take the work done at Titanium and evangelize the life-changing benefits entrepreneurs can enjoy when Magnetic Marketing principles and tactics replace the sort of wasteful and disrespectful advertising and marketing that big dumb companies (and big dumb law firms) settle for.

Together, RJon and Dan ("we") are here to offer the radical and challenging idea that just about everything you think you know and have been conditioned to believe about marketing the business of your law firm is wrong.

We're here to mute the noise and guide you to clarity about a relatively short list of fundamental marketing principles and strategies that can prevent you from being lost in a dense forest of media demanding your attention, time, and money.

If you get it, you'll smack yourself in the head for not seeing it all sooner. You'll be in awe of how much sense it makes. You'll never look at an ad, sales letter, website, or anything presuming to be "marketing" the same way again. Traditional advertising and marketing will be ruined for you.

But warning—when you do get it, you'll likely be criticized by your team, argued with by your peers, and ridiculed by even family and friends. You will need your results and a steel spine to stay strong. The outstanding results you'll see when shifting from ordinary marketing to response-driven "Magnetic Marketing" will convince you. You will need courage and discipline to stay your new course.

We promise you that being thought a "fool" or "misguided renegade" and having millions of dollars trumps being thought of as "normal" and "correct" and "proper" and barely making a living.

> Stylistic Note: As you may imagine, there's an endless array of stylistic choices an author must confront when writing a book (or a compelling brief). The authors have predominantly used the singular he, him, she, her, etc. throughout this book, rather than awkwardly saying he or she, her or him, she or he, and so on. Similarly, it's even more complicated when you're coauthoring a book and merging two voices. For the reader's convenience, and to avoid confusion because we care more about you getting the point than which of us gets credit for what, we've decided to adopt the royal "we" rather than specify "Dan said" or "RJon said."

WHERE DID THESE IDEAS ORIGINATE?

These ideas began with a discovery—or more accurately, a series of discoveries—that could well form the most important realization you'll ever arrive at as an attorney.

Because it's not enough to understand how to practice law. You also have to understand how to market so you can have clients to practice law for. In other words, you have to understand marketing. You can't just expect to be a great lawyer and therefore have that fact automatically attract clients to you. It just doesn't work like that in the real world.

Let's think about this rationally for a minute, and you'll understand just how misguided most lawyers are who brag about relying on referrals for all their business.

Law firms are mostly in the business of solving people's problems. The first thing your clients probably want to do as soon as you've solved their problem is put that problem behind them and not think about it anymore. So, it's not like they're going around looking for opportunities to tell other people about your services. At least not until we engineer a way for that to happen!

Depending on your practice area, it's likely the clients you've achieved the greatest results for are the very same ones who, left to their own devices, will go out of their way to avoid telling their friends or family about their relationship with your law firm, even if you achieved an excellent result for them. And what if you practice "happy law?" Still, it's naive to believe that evangelizing for your law firm is going to figure into the top ten, or even top one hundred, things any one of your clients is going to be thinking about on a daily basis. This is why lawyers who go around "bragging" that they settle for only having as much business as referrals may bring are either lying and in fact out doing a lot of marketing that they're just not telling you about, or they're starving for business.

If they're starving for business, a condition affecting a statistically high percentage of small law firm owners, it could be they're telling you the truth about passively waiting for the phone to ring, thereby leaving a mountain of opportunity for other law firm owners (like you), or they could be engaged in the wrong kind of marketing.

Either way, we believe that lawyers who neglect the marketing of their law firms neglect a lawyer's ethical obligation to actively market the availability of important legal services so that prospective new clients understand they have rights, options, and opportunities to have a better life.

Of course, most of the owners of struggling law firms who settle for just waiting around for the phone to ring or who rely on the crap that passes for marketing for most small law firms have likely never learned about the sort of direct-response, trackable, education-based, highly ethical, and wildly profitable "upstream" marketing you'll be exposed to in this book. So maybe we can give them a break. But the fact that YOU are reading these words right now means you are likely more entrepreneurially mature than most small law firm owners. And while they still hold on to fairy tales about "being the best leads to success," you already know that:

- ➔ You can be the most skilled practitioner in the world and still starve with no clients.
- ➔ You may have won every case you've ever tried and still starve with no new clients.
- ➔ You can have a positive attitude that Norman Vincent Peale would envy and be as motivated as a participant at a Tony Robbins seminar and still starve with no new clients.
- ➔ You can stand willing to provide great value, great service, great expertise and still starve with no new clients.
- ➔ Your law firm can literally be a paragon of virtues, with the world seemingly singing your praises twenty-four seven, and even as you bask in their applause, you can still starve!

The realization you've probably come to, which led you to this book, is this: you could very well starve, you won't get rich, and you certainly won't have peace of mind … unless and until you have an affordable, efficient, dependable means of attracting a sufficient flow of qualified LEADS and CLIENTS.

Most lawyers sort of know this, but they still focus on everything BUT the one thing that will make all the difference in the world to their success:

MARKETING

Lawyers have an ethical responsibility to market their services. People really need lawyers. The system is stacked against anyone who tries to work within the system without an attorney, even if you're smart, sophisticated, etc.

But despite all the lawyer ads everywhere you look, it's actually pretty hard for most people to hire a lawyer. Just imagine how YOU would feel sharing a whole bunch of personal and often embarrassing and intimate details of your life with a total stranger whom you only found yesterday on the internet. But lawyers, especially if you are used to dealing with very personal and private information, have a hard time fully understanding and appreciating this reality. Especially since lawyers tend to know lots of other lawyers. But the vast majority of people don't know a lawyer. They don't even know anyone who knows a lawyer!

Need proof?

Consider the fact that even a simple search on the internet produces so many advertisements for lawyers. Of course, it's possible that all those lawyers, spending all that money for all those ads, are just complete and total idiots who don't bother to track or measure ROI and don't know they're throwing their money away. And certainly that's exactly the case for many of them. But isn't it more likely that the only reason you see so many lawyers advertising so much on the internet (and elsewhere) is because even if it could work a lot better, it must be producing at least some business for them?

In other words, the fact that so many people find themselves with no better choice than to conduct a Google search to find their legal counsel is strong evidence that there are a lot of people out there who need a lawyer who don't know a lawyer and don't even know anyone who knows a lawyer—why else resort to hiring a total stranger? And so we believe lawyers have an ethical obligation to proactively market the availability of legal services because no one struggling with the sorts of issues (or even opportunities) that call for the services of a lawyer ought to have to ALSO worry about "Where do I find someone to help me, whom I can trust?" while they're smack-dab in the middle of their problem or opportunity!

Magnetic Marketing helps lawyers who embrace it to live up to the ethical obligation all lawyers should take seriously to ensure that when a prospective new client needs a lawyer, he or she already knows a lawyer and can feel comfortable sharing all the sensitive information a lawyer generally needs access to in order to provide great representation.

Magnetic Marketing also addresses the fiduciary responsibilities all law firm owners have to all those who are depending on the business to remain viable—by giving you the tools to create an asset in your business that generates a steady stream of prospective new clients and instills the confidence you need to decline engagements from the wrong clients or even from the right clients when they bring you the wrong kinds of cases.

When built, tested, refined, and proven to work—day in, day out—even when you're not there working, your Magnetic Marketing Machine™ will become one of the most valuable assets of your law firm, which you can likely sell for two to three times profit when the time comes to sell your law firm.

Paradoxically, though, when you do get a good Magnetic Marketing Machine working for your law firm and it's producing new clients year in and year out, quarter in and quarter out, month in and month out, week in and week out, day in and day out—without you having to be there chained to your desk, turning the wheel yourself—you may discover why members of How to Manage a Small Law Firm say, "Happy Lawyers Make More Money," and then maybe you won't be so excited about selling such a good thing!

Thus it is critical to understand that many of the frustrations and internal problems you're likely experiencing with your firm today are because you DON'T have a good Marketing Machine or System. Many law firms stand ready to provide great services, delivered by caring lawyers with noble motivations. But they fail because they don't have enough sales opportunities. To paraphrase Thoreau, most lawyers lead lives of quiet desperation because they don't know how to create a steady and sufficient supply of qualified clients.

Therefore, for the rest of this book, please refrain from thinking of yourself as a lawyer. If you put this book down, please refrain from telling anyone that you're an attorney before you pick it up again. Refrain from saying that you have a law firm. Because that's not what this book is about. We want to help you give yourself a *promotion* and help you begin thinking of yourself as a business owner and as an entrepreneur who owns a business that happens to be a law firm. An entrepreneurial law firm owner who has made the courageous decision to step away from (the above) conventional thinking about law firm marketing and take the road less traveled.

IT'S TIME FOR A DIFFERENT VISION

You'll discover that one of the greatest gifts of *Magnetic Marketing* is the shift in mindset and vision it enables. Once you shift your mindset, a whole new world becomes accessible to you.

The principles in this book have been taught in various forms since the mid-1970s and have been tested over and again by attorneys of all shapes, sizes, practice areas, and locations who use them to create a steady flow of new clients. These principles work in consumer as well as business law, and throughout this book you'll discover how attorneys just like you have used the very same strategies to grow, scale, and differentiate their law firms—to rise above the competition and to quickly demand (and receive) top dollar for their services.

We're here to give you the entire vision plus the architecture that will allow you to make this vision a reality—of being the prosperous owner of a law firm that's a REAL business, not of random or episodic income events, not of endless need for the next new client, not of frequent worry where the next appointment might come from.

The vision of certainty and security and stability. Of a continuous and steady inflow of desired clients who trust your firm, rely on your firm, and refer their friends, family, and/or business acquaintances to your firm. Even of creating equity and wealth, not just day-to-day income.

A vision that does NOT require any special background—just the commitment to use what you discover. You can apply it to any kind of practice serving any kind of market; in fact, you'll soon meet lawyers in this book who will demonstrate exactly how this SYSTEM worked for them.

For now, know that YOU CAN turbocharge your law firm's ability to magnetically attract and achieve with what you'll discover in the following pages.

Let's begin.

PS—You do NOT need to read this entire book before also taking some next steps to connect with Magnetic Marketing for Lawyers. Feel free to take advantage of the invitations on the next page NOW.

Visit us online to access these valuable resources:

Register your book

To receive a free audiobook PLUS our Magnetic Marketing Toolkit, which contains valuable downloads and worksheets to help you create your own Magnetic Marketing System in your law firm, visit

➔ MagneticMarketingForLawyers.com/Register.

Test Your Magnetic Marketing Status

Curious about where you are on the Magnetic Marketing spectrum? Most law firms are doing marketing, but few are magnetically attracting clients with a fail-proof system.

➔ Take the Magnetic Marketing Quiz to find out at MagneticMarketingForLawyers.com/SelfTest.

The Magnetic Marketing System and Toolkit

First released twenty-five years ago, the Magnetic Marketing System and Toolkit has been the best-selling training kit for entrepreneurial attorneys who are interested in magnetically attracting their very best clients.

➔ Invest in the system at MagneticMarketingForLawyers.com/System.

FOUNDATIONS OF MAGNETIC MARKETING

CHAPTER 1

What If Everything You've Ever Been Told about Growing Your Law Firm Was Wrong?

Sorry to say this, but you have been lied to for a very long time!

Note the nonuse of softer words like "misled," "misinformed," "offered less than optimal advice." Nope. Let's lay it out straight and plain.

You've been lied to.

It's critical to your success that you open your eyes to this fact and the blunt, unvarnished truth about what entrepreneurial law firm owners do to attract the best clients, which struggling lawyers don't. Frankly, not everyone is ready for such a conversation. Many prefer excuses to achievement. Others prefer fantasy to reality.

The SYSTEM revealed in this book will radically alter how your law firm acquires clients and boost your firm's revenues dramatically. It pulls back the curtain on real-world strategies that are already being used and that have transformed already hundreds of seemingly "ordinary" law firms—in a wide range of practice areas—into extraordinary client-attracting machines that far outperform legal industry norms, peers, competitors, and even, at first, the wildest imagination of their owner(s).

How did they do it?

By making the strategic switch from traditional advertising, marketing, and client development to a response-driven marketing strategy we call "***Magnetic Marketing.***"

Magnetic Marketing for Lawyers was created to help ordinary attorneys like you—perhaps with NO marketing knowledge or expertise—and empower them to create compelling marketing on their own without needing to hire outside help.

Magnetic Marketing has impacted lawyers across the planet, literally changing the way clients are obtained. Indeed, today they form what could well be called a "secret society" of ambitious and entrepreneurial law firm owners who have discovered that Magnetic Marketing enables them to create massively profitable law firms that are FUN to run and MUCH more profitable than poorly run law firms that require the owner to suffer and sacrifice and sweat.

Its roots go back many, many decades, if not centuries. Its core foundational principle is that every advertisement, promotion, email, flyer, TV commercial, speech, published article, etc. focuses ALL energy on:

- ➔ **Targeting the ideal client, and**
- ➔ **Getting them to respond in a specific way—not wasting any effort on branding, image, humor, style, or anything else unless it increases the response rate by your firm's ideal client.**

THIS is the kind of marketing discussed in this book—marketing designed to "magnetically attract" in a specific, repeatable, predictable, and measurable way. If you want to have a more successful law firm, then this is the ONLY model of marketing that you should invest your precious time in and use. Magnetic Marketing is also highly ethical and professional. In fact, when done right, Magnetic Marketing far exceeds all standards of bar rules that we have found in this country.

HERE'S THE KEY FACT ABOUT THE BUSINESS OF A LAW FIRM THAT YOU MUST EMBRACE ...

Without a sufficient and steady stream of clients with whom your law firm can exchange valuable legal services for money, nothing else about your law firm really matters.

Not your most impressive professional credentials, not the esteem of your peers or any of your past professional accomplishments. Not your hardworking "nose-to-the-grindstone" ethic. Not your most excellent website. Not your high visibility location. None of this helps one single client, or you, if it doesn't cause prospective new clients to find and hire your law firm to help them solve their problems.

Being more educated or talented or skilled or more willing than others has ZERO value if your law firm has no clients. And the chance of you showing up for your clients as the best version of yourself if you're losing sleep over where the next client will come from shortchanges all concerned.

Many attorneys harm themselves and others—including their clients—by denying this reality. They desperately want to believe that better is better ... having better credentials ... having gone to a better law school ... having more or better experience ... having more integrity ... better work ethic ... having paid your dues ... investing in better technology and tools ... even being a better lawyer! BETTER *SHOULD* BE ENOUGH. And lest we get into an argument about this—we totally agree! Better SHOULD be enough.

Perhaps in an idyllic and just world that would be so.

But not in THIS world.

In this world you are not automatically awarded what you deserve or think you deserve. It's not a pure meritocracy. If that were the case, there'd probably be no rich criminals and no poor lawyers.

Successful law firm owners know money moves about for its own reasons, and neither need nor deservingness are magnetic to it. Instead, it depends on powerful, well-crafted, measurable strategies—a tried and true system—that work across all kinds of media.

At this point you're either "getting it" or else (sadly) you may be like most struggling lawyers who keep experiencing undesirable results in their business but still refuse to consider the possibility that what they were told by law school professors, employers, and mentors about the business of running a successful law firm was just plain wrong.

Fortunately, even in this first chapter, this book has already exposed you to—and we'll continue to press—the point that there is a better way to generate business for a law firm, and it's called: *Magnetic Marketing*. This kind of marketing is as proven as any of the natural laws because it is rooted in the laws of nature. Unlike laws made by men, the laws of nature are nonnegotiable, and you can't appeal them. While you can ignore them (and many do), you cannot ignore the consequences of ignoring natural law, though many try. Too many struggling law firm owners trained and skilled at the practice of law attempt, at their peril, to "lawyer" the laws of nature upon which Magnetic Marketing is based. But you cannot negotiate with the wind. You can harness it and let it work for you, though.

A much more effective strategy than continuing to ignore it when your law firm produces undesirable results year after year is to change your actions and let Magnetic Marketing begin working for you. Let the wind work for you instead of pushing so hard against it.

We tell you all of this now because it may require some patience from you and some practice to stop thinking about all of this like a lawyer and let yourself think as an entrepreneur.

This switch is critical because …

YOU'VE BEEN SET UP TO STRUGGLE ENDLESSLY

As the owner of a small or solo law firm, you face the constant pressure of having far too much to do and never enough time to get it all done.

If you're not careful, you can get caught in a trap with growing stress from year to year because of the demands coming at you from seemingly every direction—client attraction, sales, managing case progress, hiring, training, managing, and making sure your firm is making a profit with staff, anticipating and maintaining the physical part of the business, including (especially) the firm's intellectual property and financial controls so you don't wind up growing the top line but forget to take anything home from the bottom to feed your family. Oh, and then there's the substantive practice of law too.

It's all an endless challenge—or rather an interrelated set of challenges—that law school simply did not equip you for. Which is why most solo and small law firm owners feel trapped. Because they are trapped.[2]

The way out is through Magnetic Marketing.

Here's what we mean …

Let's just take a very typical example of a very capable attorney

---

2 Is it any surprise that among the many other "truths" about what it takes to build and sustain a highly successful law firm, the powers that be may have also neglected to properly educate you about how to market your law firm? Consider that law schools are mostly endowed by big law firms. And big law firms have a big need for relatively cheap labor whose work product can be marked up and sold for usually a 3–5x profit. The last thing management of a big law firm wants is for their associates to be empowered to open up their own successful law firm and keep the profits for themselves. Plus, when's the last time you met a law school professor who owned and operated a highly successful law firm?

running his or her own firm—if you think the practice area matters, you're missing the point, so please don't. Let's say this lawyer is ready, willing, and able to work 10 hours a day x 5 days a week x 50 weeks a year. Of course, you already know this doesn't mean our hypothetical solo lawyer is *billing* 10 hours a day. Instead this very busy but still-struggling lawyer probably prioritizes time as follows:

1. Do whatever legal work he or she can—maybe 4 hours a day—because if you don't do the work in front of you, then clients complain and you starve.
2. Put out management "fires" in the firm—probably 2 hours a day.
3. Get around to sending out some bills—this lawyer probably takes about half an hour per day to account for (make guesses about) the "billable" work done in between everything else coming at him or her throughout the day.
4. Meeting with prospective new clients—maybe 1–2 hours a day, except usually the prospective new clients haven't been prequalified, preeducated, or preconditioned to engage the firm, so conversion rates are unpredictable, which leads to a lot of demoralizing inefficiency.
5. Marketing usually happens as an afterthought whenever the well appears to be getting dry—the nonstrategic, unbudgeted, and likely random episodic events of marketing probably average out to about 1–2 hours a day.

Total hours: 10 hours a day.

And there you have it, a recipe for getting and staying stuck.

Now let's follow the money …

Let's assume the lawyer from our example bills by the hour and manages to actually collect all 4 hours a day that he or she bills x 5 days x 50 weeks—that's 1,000 hours per year. With a billing rate of $250/hour, this law firm is going to max out at just $250,000 per year, and that assumes all "billables" are in fact billed and collected, which is unlikely.

If your firm works on a contingency fee basis and if you manage it well, then you have an expectation for the amount of revenue every hour of legal work production should generate. Let's assume the lawyer from our example expects to generate around $2,500 for every 10 hours of legal work invested into a case. That's a "realization rate" of still about $250/hour. Switching our hypothetical lawyer to a contingency fee billing arrangement still doesn't change the fact that without a reliable marketing plan, sales system, well-trained and well-managed staff, and documented systems used to operate the business, the lawyer who may even take pride in "doing it all" is still only likely able to devote about 4 hours a day to substantive legal work. And assuming this lawyer is willing (and even able) to keep up the pace of 10-hour days x 5 days x 50 weeks, we're still looking at a struggling law firm whose owner is wearing all the hats to gross around $250,000 per year.

And you may have noticed, the owner of both law firms described above is on the road to burnout. Because working 10 hours a day, 5 days a week, 50 weeks a year is unsustainable and unrealistic. But let's say there's some superhuman lawyer out there whose family is willing to go along with this sort of plan with no end in sight. After overhead, the owner of this firm is still only taking home between

$100,000–$150,000 per year, at least until our superlawyer hits the wall and it all falls apart.

Sadly, there's no end in sight for this lawyer. No escape, no time off, no vacations, no sick days, no leverage, no sustainability. Life sucks. And everyone involved pays a price—the lawyer, the family of this lawyer, and the clients too because their lawyer isn't showing up as the best version of himself or herself. How could anyone?

Now perhaps you've managed to do better than this. Good for you. If your law firm is already doing better than most, you're probably already pretty excited about learning how to apply the principles of *Magnetic Marketing for Lawyers* to take your law firm to even greater heights in terms of revenue, predictability, and freedom for yourself!

And if your law firm has been stuck in the first stage of growth (from $0 to about $250,000) for more than a few years, at least now you know why and can give yourself a break. Now you know it has nothing to do with your skills as a lawyer or your commitment to your clients. Once you put the principles of Magnetic Marketing to work for your law firm, you too will soon find you're going to have more free time, better conversion rates with prospective new clients, and more confidence about investing back some of your newfound free time and extra income to build a better law firm that works for you!

In case you're wondering, here's about how the income levels of solo lawyers and owners of single-shareholder small law firms with typically five lawyers or fewer tend to "spread out" in most markets and across most practice areas:

- ➔ 1 percent use their law firm to create tremendous income and wealth
- ➔ 4 percent do very well

- 15 percent earn a good living
- 60 percent struggle endlessly
- 20 percent fail

Yes, it's true. In every market and all practice areas, there are some solo and small law firm owners who are using their law firms to have a much bigger positive impact on the world, and they're creating tremendous income and wealth for themselves, too, in the process. And in those very same cities, practicing in exactly the same area of the law, there are some very good practitioners who are presently failing and would gladly take a job if offered.

More to the point, what you've got to know is that nearly 80 percent of the solo and small law firm owners you're going to meet at any bar function are struggling financially and in so many other ways, too, because of the low income and inconsistent revenues of their law firm, and only 15 percent are actually earning a good living. This is important for you to know because what passes for "normal" or "acceptable" for the vast majority of solo and small law firm owners doesn't have to be what YOU accept for your standards. You can choose to adopt the standards demanded by the top 5 percent of solo and small law firm owners. Just don't expect to meet many of them rubbing elbows with everyone else at many bar functions ... because eagles tend to prefer the company of other eagles.

OK, we knew when we decided to adapt Dan's book for lawyers that this would be an issue. RJon said, "They're going to want proof." So, if you need more proof, here's what you can do to find it for yourself.

Make plans to attend a few different bar functions, or log onto a few of the lawyer discussion groups you can find online and conduct this test for yourself. Begin by complaining about how "tough" things are for you in your law firm. Complain that there aren't enough clients, that the clients you do have don't pay and you're working too many hours. Now, if you were among eagles, they'd either swoop down and try to lift you up or else they'd just fly away to avoid getting trapped. But if you've been to many bar functions or waste too much time pecking around with the chickens online, then you already know what results you'll find. Before you know it, you'll be inundated with useless bits of advice, plenty of commiseration, and invitations to join a chorus of stories, rationalizations, and excuses for why things have to be that way.

But that wasn't the test. This is the test. Ask any of them to explain their marketing strategy. Ask them to describe, in detail, whom their marketing strategy has been designed to resonate with and whom it has been equally designed to repel and protect them from. Ask them what measurements they're using to track ROI and hold their vendors accountable. Ask about having a marketing budget committed for the next twelve months and financial projections they're basing that budget upon. Ask what the average gross margin is on the services their marketing is designed to sell. Ask if they even know what a gross margin is. Or cost of goods sold. Ask what KPIs they use to track overall performance of their business or even just the profitability of their marketing. Ask if they have a written business plan that explains in plain English how any of The 7 Main Parts of a Successful Law Firm™ are supposed to operate in their law firm to deliver quality services for clients and profits back to them.

OK, that was RJon, the cofounder and CEO of How to Manage a Small Law Firm on a bit of a rant with that last paragraph. You can visit HowtoManage.com/Magnetic7MainParts to learn more about

The 7 Main Parts of a Successful Law Firm. This book is about the first of the 7 Main Parts: Marketing. So, when you conduct your test, just ask the loudest and most persuasive of the complainers to explain to you in plain English what the marketing strategy is for his or her struggling law firm, and we're pretty confident we already know what you're going to get.

Part of the problem is that most solo and small law firm owners believe they have to tolerate living the way they are living because that's the way they see that so many other solo and small law firm owners tolerate living their lives too.

Most of them believe they must continue to tolerate living that way because they think the only way out is to advertise and market the way they've seen done by big law firms—so they waste lots of money and time chasing so many different kinds of media to promote image, brand, and presence. And when that doesn't work, they reach the wrong conclusion about what is or isn't possible, instead of the correct conclusion that they may simply need to find a better way that is more appropriate for a small law firm.

You simply cannot build, and you certainly won't sustain the success of, your law firm if you make the mistake of trying to keep up with the Joneses or jumping into media because "that's what the big-name law firms are doing."

Big-name law firms have all sorts of reasons for the way they advertise and market that have ZERO to do with what it takes for a small law firm to get a client.

Your agenda is much simpler—in fact, there's a huge difference between how BIG law firms use marketing and how you as the owner of a small law firm must learn to think about it:

Big Law Firm Agenda for Advertising and Marketing

1. Please/appease partners (most of whom have no data, but lots of opinions).
2. Impress lawyers outside of the firm, most of whom know zip about advertising or marketing and have no way of knowing if the marketing is even working or not.
3. Intimidate lawyers who work for the firm into believing they can't make it on their own without a big advertising budget so they'll stay.
4. Provide "cover" for decision-makers at big dumb companies who need to be able to defend their hiring decision ("Don't blame me, I hired the biggest-name firm in town").
5. Use as a recruiting tool to establish prestige, especially for law firms that have a tendency to churn through a lot of associates due to "up or out," high billable quotas, toxic work environments, etc. ("My son-in-law works for that law firm.")
6. Unify partners in far-flung offices so everyone feels like they're working for the same firm. (This is actually a legitimate management and recruiting objective of advertising and marketing ... let's schedule a strategy session via HowToManage.com/MagneticBigFirm to discuss this point once your firm has so many offices and so many partners that nobody knows each other!)
7. Sell something.

YOUR Small Law Firm's Agenda

1. Book an appointment; sell services. NOW!

Big law firms may have the wherewithal to use sloppy, wasteful, "mass advertising" practices that hemorrhage money left and right.

This unfortunately leads many of your peers to "model" those same ideas, what they saw/read/heard every day, wrongly thinking that "if it works for them, it's gotta work for us too."

Here's the No BS Truth: The typical attorney is essentially clueless when it comes to advertising and marketing. This makes them highly vulnerable to becoming "Advertising Victims"—easy prey for media salespeople and ad agencies and anyone else who doesn't know how to actually close the deal and make a sale.

Don't believe it?

Corner one or two of your peers, try to get them to tell you with confidence WHERE their firm's clients come from, what it costs to get a client, what kind of results does one ad get versus another. Try. They can't. They're guessing. And that's what the advertising industry vultures rely on. They don't want to be held accountable for results! But we believe you deserve a saner, more productive path to growth that makes your life more pleasant, lucrative, and certain.

IT'S NOT ABOUT WORKING HARDER

You've been told over and over again the answer to all your troubles is to:

- ➔ Work Harder
- ➔ Work Smarter
- ➔ Become a Better Lawyer

Sorry, but none of those will fly or even come close to hitting the mark.

It's not about working harder. As we've already seen with the example earlier, there aren't many more hours left to give if you're already stuck in the trap of working for your law firm. And it's not about becoming a better lawyer either. That's not going to magically attract more clients to your firm! You don't need more hard work. And you probably don't need to become a better lawyer in order to magnetize your law firm's marketing to attract more and better clients. Instead, you need a NEW strategy. A smarter strategy. You need a SYSTEM—one that works for you 24/7/365, doing all this for you:

- ➔ A system that generates a predictable flow of new clients to your doorstep
- ➔ A system that turns every client into two additional clients
- ➔ A system that creates repeatable business
- ➔ A system that allows you more financial

freedom and time to think about how to manage your law firm more like a business and less like just a practice

- ➔ A system focused on marketing

The more productive answer is to develop a SYSTEM that attracts new clients to your firm in an organized way.

YOU MIGHT NOW BE WONDERING ...

"I'm already working events, getting referrals, and getting clients on my own. Why would I need this Magnetic Marketing stuff?"

Consider the legend of John Henry—a story about a man in the 1800s whose prowess with the railroad hammer made him a legend.

John Henry could swing a hammer like no one else. He could drive a railroad spike with one massive swing of the hammer and drive more spikes straight into the ground in an hour than anyone else could.

John Henry was a big, muscular, skilled athlete of a hammer swinger, and everyone admired him greatly because of how much work he could do in an hour. Just like everyone may admire you today in your law firm or in your peer group because of how much capacity for work you have. And how much legal work you can produce in an hour. And how many clients you can produce in an hour of networking or speechmaking or article writing.

You are a Rainmaker! All Hail the Rainmaker of The Firm!

Well, we're here to tell you the age of the Rainmaker is over because someone invented a steam hammer.

A steam hammer would get rolled down the track from spike to spike. A lever would get pulled or a button pushed, and boom, boom, boom, the machine would drive a steel spike into the ground almost as fast as John Henry could with just one of his mighty swings!

So, one day, as legend has it, a competition was organized, John Henry versus the Steam Hammer, to see who could get further in a day.

You know who won?

John Henry won because John Henry is a legend!

Your rainmaking skills may be the stuff of legend too. You may be better than anyone at getting clients. Maybe you get all the business you do because of how great you are.

The only problem is at the end of the day, John Henry dropped dead of a heart attack with a hammer in his hand, just like maybe you're going to drop dead of a heart attack because all client acquisition depends on how great you are.

Now get this ...

A mediocre marketing machine will outperform the most brilliant marketer in the world EVERY time.

This book will get you out of the railroad tunnel, get you out of the role of rainmaker, and help you build a Magnetic Marketing Machine that will keep doing the marketing for you day in and day out, week in and week out, month in and month out.

You want to go on vacation? No problem. The machine is going to keep chugging along. You get sick? No problem. The machine is going to keep chugging along. A loved one needs you to come to their aid and you'll never forgive yourself if you can't be there for him or her? No problem. The marketing machine is going to keep chugging along. The marketing machine is just going to keep chugging along.

That's what Magnetic Marketing can do for you.

Use of the word "transformative" would not risk overstatement.

WARNING: Chances are your thinking has already begun to change about how you want to be marketing your law firm and living your life.

As we continue to explain and reveal the Magnetic Marketing for Lawyers System, there's a very good chance you're going to experience a quantum leap in terms of how you think about every part of how you want to manage the business of your law firm.

As much as we'd love it if you'd immediately run out and tell everyone you know about *Magnetic Marketing for Lawyers*, please don't do that just yet. Because they won't understand. And you won't have the proof you may need to withstand the onslaught of doubts and criticism you'll likely encounter when you share new ideas that challenge the beliefs that so many (struggling) law firm owners have about how to market their business.

Instead, give yourself a chance to implement the Magnetic Marketing System for your own law firm, and let it begin producing amazing results for you. Then you won't have to explain or defend as much to the lawyers you're trying to help.

And then we'll have a different conversation about why most of them will STILL ignore what you say and keep repeating what's not currently working out very well for them—and never will.

WHY NOW IS THE RIGHT TIME FOR THIS NEW SYSTEM

You want a system that enables you to better target the most appropriate and valuable clients for your firm so you're not wasting time, energy, resources scurrying down rabbit holes chasing "would-be" clients who in fact will "never be." A system that gives you reliable and predictable results so you finally know when you invest X dollars, you can expect Y number of leads, then Z number of appointments or selling opportunities. Most importantly, you need a system you can comprehend and control.

It's just too complicated to wing it on your own now. Technology is great. When operated by competent professionals who are held to objective standards based on measured performance, technology can work wonders for your law firm. A poorly conceived marketing plan powered by modern technology can also burn through a pile of your money more quickly today than ever before. You never really could succeed with a haphazard approach. But nowadays the dangers of having a haphazard approach are greater than ever before.

You MUST follow a well-conceived, testable, scalable, practical system—and you've come to the right place to discover such a system for you. Best of all, it does NOT require any sort of fancy technology to make it work. In fact, lawyers have been using the principles and the system described in this book for hundreds of years to build highly successful law firms.

WELCOME TO "THE UNIVERSITY OF HARSH REALITY"

If you've read this far and not run away, then welcome and congratulations! You could consider this book a university of sorts—a tough one, to be sure, because reality and life have always been harsh. As Hollywood legend John Wayne once said:

"Life is hard. And it's harder if you're stupid."

Lawyers obviously aren't "stupid" when it comes to raw cerebral horsepower. The problem lies in the "stupid" things lawyers do that they have been led to believe are necessary truths about the business of how to manage a small law firm.

That may seem a bit blunt or even a bit uncomfortable. Good.

This book was written to offer the blunt, unvarnished truth about how you really CAN create a flood of new clients while building wealth, independence, and sustainability into your business.

There are a lot of numbers bandied about in marketing—response percentages, circulation, pass-along effect, visitors, dedicated visitors, likes, friends, fans, followers, and on and on. Sorry, but it's all BS. Only one number really matters when it comes to law firm marketing:

It's all about leads that convert to income. Period.

But one can also be the very worst number in business. If you are overly dependent on any ONE thing in your business, you will—at some point—be punished for this vulnerability. You can bank on that. One key team member, one key account or client, one service, one skill, one technology—all woefully insecure and unstable. This is particularly true of MEDIA. (Can anyone say, "Google Penguin"?)

The key to making your law firm into a magnetic, robust, and economy-proof client attraction machine is developing multiple channels. Later in this book, we'll describe them as "mini oil wells." *Magnetic Marketing for Lawyers* isn't about "one big thing." It's about one way of thinking and acting as we show you how to design, build, and test lots of little things that work together to make your law firm magnetic to the right kinds of clients with the right kinds of cases and protect you and your staff from the rest.

The foundational key to making this happen …

YOU MUST SEPARATE YOURSELF FROM THE COMPETITION

You must make yourself the go-to authority and, better yet, make your law firm the go-to authority for some audience that faces a specific problem. And the primary way to accomplish this is by crafting an answer to this question:

"Why should I choose you and your law firm versus any and every other option to obtain the very same service to solve the very same problem?"

Resolved with what legendary ad man Rosser Reeves called a *USP*, a *Unique Selling Proposition.*

Tremendous turnarounds in business have taken place as the result of great USPs. Domino's Pizza was originally driven by a marketing message that everybody came to know, *"Fresh hot pizza delivered in 30 minutes or less, guaranteed."*

If you dissect it, you'll see some interesting things.

First of all, it doesn't claim to be all things to all people. There's no mention of Mama's recipe from the old country. No mention of a special sauce. In fact, there's not even any mention of *good* pizza. All it says is that it is going to get to you while it's still hot and it's still fresh and that they guarantee to do that.

You must make yourself the go-to authority and, better yet, make your law firm the go-to authority for some audience that faces a specific problem.

What is your USP? This is going to take a little bit of work. Somewhere in your firm, there is a good answer. If not, you need to make one.

There are two different extremes most struggling law firm owners go to when we start to talk about Unique Selling Proposition.

First is to jump to the conclusion that there is nothing special about them. "I'm just like all the other lawyers in my area who provide basically the same sort of services." The other extreme is to take unwarranted comfort in being "better" than all the other lawyers in town.

Well, sometimes, in rare instances, that's true. Maybe your firm really is exactly like all the rest. Or maybe you really are the best.

But none of that matters. Because what's going to make your firm's marketing more effective isn't bragging about being the best. Notwithstanding the fact that bar rules prohibit this, everyone's doing it. And when everyone is saying the same thing, it's sort of the same thing as everyone saying nothing. That's why Rosser didn't call it a "Best-Selling Proposition." Instead, we have to carve out what's going to make your firm unique, as in, different.

Here are three questions you can ask yourself to help kick-start the process of finding or creating your firm's USP.

1) What specifically do you do that's truly different compared to competitors?

For Domino's, it was originally being there in thirty minutes or less. More recently, they revolutionized the company against badly sagging sales by taking the worst ranked pizza to the best ranked for taste and quality. But that's actually upping the ante on already being in the game.

2) How do you uniquely benefit your target market?

J. K. Rowling of the *Harry Potter* books and her publisher made each new book's release of exceptional benefit to independent bookstores with a devised plan for big events, books held back to release at midnight, drawing huge numbers of kids and parents into these stores milling about at a party, in costume, snacking and browsing and buying other books for an hour or more before the clock struck midnight.

The target market, the bookstore owner, was uniquely benefited in reciprocity. Rowling got far more promotional work out of the store owners than hundreds of other authors of other children's fantasy books.

3) Can you niche your target market in a way nobody else can or will?

One student of Magnetic Marketing, a lawyer named Bill Hammond, created Alzheimer's Law—a subset of elder law essentially wrapping traditional estate planning, Medicare and Medicaid planning, and other family legal matters inside a differently described package, positioned for families with a senior showing signs of or having been diagnosed with dementia. This enabled Bill to use the exact lead generation strategies laid out in this system.

Another lawyer named Carrie Shultz created Fathers' Rights Divorce out of a "normal" family law firm by creating special programs that cater to the unique challenges of dads who need to file or respond to a divorce. Admittedly, 80 percent of what Carrie's firm does is the same as what would be called for if representing a mother going through a divorce or even a man or a woman with no children. But if you're a father facing the prospect of divorce, the 20 percent "difference" could make 100 percent of the difference, and so more than $2 million worth of business is now magnetized to Carrie's law firm every year.

A third example to get your creative juices flowing is The Patent Professor, founded by attorney John Rizvi, whose intellectual property law firm does indeed offer high quality patent, trademark, and other intellectual property services. But when John had the opportunity to serve as an adjunct professor at his local law school, he discovered, to his delight, that he really enjoyed educating people about intellectual property. Today more than $5 million per year of mostly individual inventor clients appreciate the unique educational approach John built into his law firm, and we track subscribers to his educational and entertaining video channel as a reliable "leading indicator" of next quarter's and next year's revenues.

How to Manage a Small Law Firm manages hundreds of law firms with an impressive track record of growth, and so it is with much experience that we say there's no need to allow your law firm to be perceived by the market as like every other law firm, only "better" or, worse, "cheaper." Take the time to create your own USP—it's one of the greatest marketing weapons you can ever have for your law firm.

Go to MagneticMarketingForLawyers.com/USP to watch a bonus lesson about how to craft your firm's USP.

CHAPTER 2

Why So Much Law Firm Marketing Fails

Over the course of this book, you're already beginning to discover a totally new and different way to market legal services.

In fact, you could consider this "an alternative universe" of marketing, where all the fundamentals you thought were true have been turned on their head. Kind of like that episode in *Star Trek* where Captain Kirk was a bad guy and Spock sported an eminently logical goatee.[3] Except the mirror universe this book gives you passage into is so much better than the one most lawyers know and tolerate for their businesses and careers.

It's important that you set aside any preconceptions you might have about changing gears with your marketing because the fact of the matter is clear and has been for years:

"Most of the advertising and marketing done by attorneys STINKS."

Monstrous sums are wasted and opportunities lost. Even amid all the change in technology and practically limitless options available to get your message out, nothing has changed for the better. In fact, if anything, it has gotten worse.

---

3 "Mirror, Mirror" is the fourth episode of the second season; it was first broadcast on October 6, 1967. The episode involves a transporter malfunction that swaps Captain Kirk and his companions with their evil counterparts from a parallel universe. In this "mirror universe," the *Enterprise* is a ship of the Terran Empire, a conquering and murdering organization where officers are assassinated as punishment and as a means of promotion. This episode has been noted for introducing the concept of the mirror universe in the *Star Trek* franchise.

Lawyers are really confused and overwhelmed—told they must do this, that, the other thing, more and more, just to get the same results.

To clear away the confusion, here's a relatively short list of mistakes that, when understood and corrected, can safeguard your sanity from the assault of a thousand points of media options demanding your attention, time, and money.

MISTAKE #1: MOST LAWYERS CONFUSE MARKETING AND SALES

There are *7 Main Parts of a Successful Law Firm*™. There are also *7 Main Parts of a Struggling Law Firm*™. The difference between the successful law firms and the law firms that are struggling has much more to do with ignorance, confusion, and inattention to most of these 7 main parts than how good a lawyer anyone is in the law firm.

RJon's business, How to Manage a Small Law Firm, helps hundreds of—perhaps by the time you read this, more than one thousand—solo and small law firm owners manage and keep each of the *7 Main Parts of a Successful Law Firm* in alignment.[4] But this book is focused on the foundational first of those parts of a successful law firm, Marketing, and we touch upon sales a bit, too. That's because if your firm's marketing does its job well then sales is simplified and more efficient, which is an important detail to keep in mind. But too many lawyers confuse the two concepts and it doesn't help that lawyers use euphemisms like "Business Development" and "Rainmaker" to describe roles that encompass components of both Marketing and Sales. So here it is:

---

4 Visit HowtoManage.com/Magnetic7MainParts to learn more about *7 Main Parts of a Successful Law Firm*

Marketing is everything that happens to get the right clients with the right kinds of cases to the right place at the right time in the right quantity. They should arrive for their initial consultation already prequalified, preeducated, preconditioned, and, therefore, predisposed to engage your law firm when they arrive in person, by telephone, via a web meeting, or through whatever new technology is invented next after the publication of this book. Sadly, people who don't know anything about marketing all too often mistakenly believe media or technology alone can be a substitute for actual marketing strategy.

Many lawyers are surprised to know that part of the job of Marketing is also to screen out and protect the firm's resources from being consumed by the wrong kind of prospective new clients or even great prospective new clients who happen to have the wrong sort of case or matter for any given law firm. And more than a few struggling lawyers have been upset at the notion that part of the job of Marketing is also to regulate the flow of prospective new clients coming in at the top of the funnel in order to protect the firm's reputation and cash flow by not overwhelming production capacity. If a person is dying of thirst in a desert, it's understandable that the notion of having too much of a good thing might be foreign to him or her.

A Magnetic Marketing System allows you to align the flow of prospective new clients with the firm's capacity to serve them all, which is part of the "secret" for how we maximize the lifetime value of our relationship with each client, turning one into two, and so much more.

Sales (when done the right way) is an ethical, professional, predictable, and highly profitable system for helping prospective new clients think through and get clarity about where they are today with their situation versus where they would prefer to be tomorrow versus where they would like to avoid being tomorrow if they don't get some help.

Unfortunately, most prospective new clients walk into a law firm with important problems and walk out of the law firm with the same important problems still unresolved. This is because most lawyers have never been trained how to professionally and ethically sell legal services. Also, unfortunately, for even more prospective new clients, most lawyers don't understand—as you now do—what marketing actually is, and so they rely too heavily on sales instead of creating a marketing machine and letting it do its job.

Consider this. Dan is an excellent salesperson, truly world-class. RJon is about the best around, too, at selling professional services. And we've each personally sold many tens of millions of dollars' worth of products and professional services. Plus, we've each trained legions of highly effective sales professionals who have themselves sold into the many hundreds of millions of dollars' worth of professional services. Dan has even written books on the subject, and RJon's company earns millions of dollars per year just training nonattorneys how to professionally, ethically, and very profitably sell legal services for the small law firms that send them for the training each year.

So, you might expect us to rely more heavily than either of us actually does in our own businesses on salespeople. Instead, we each go to great lengths to build better marketing machines so we can be less dependent on having the most amazing salespeople in the world.

Salespeople can quit; sales machines cannot. They'll never have a bad day, and they'll never tell you "the leads are weak," at least not without objective data to prove it!

MISTAKE #2: MARKETING TO THE WRONG PEOPLE

Most lawyers market to the wrong people. When their marketing fails to deliver, they blame it on something else. It's not fancy enough. It's not big enough. I didn't get to tell them enough about my credentials. It uses the wrong technology. And, our favorite, I abdicated to the wrong vendor to do my thinking for me! This is not to say that any of these factors ISN'T a problem. They very well could play a role in any ad's success or lack thereof.

But the bigger problem is the simple fact that most lawyer advertising is not directed at a person; instead, it's directed at the PROBLEM.

This is understandable. Lawyers are trained to solve problems. Spot the issue. Analyze the fact pattern. Apply the law. Solve the problem. Oh, wait a second, what's that you say? I need to find a person who has this problem and help him find the courage and the motivation to solve it before I can get busy doing my important legal work? Most lawyers treat client acquisition as an afterthought, a nuisance, something that has to get done so that we can get on with the important legal work. We believe that helping a person learn about his or her options and find clarity, courage, and the motivation to take a positive step in their life by deciding to get help is important work too.

You can do this test and spot the problem for yourself. In fact, by now you'll probably have a hard time NOT seeing this problem everywhere you see a law firm burning piles of cash on so-called "marketing." Open up any newspaper, drive down any highway, do a search on any web browser, and notice what almost all of the law firm advertising has in common. It's all speaking to a problem. Hardly any of it speaks to a person. "Do you have this problem? Call us. We're the best."

Remember, people don't hire law firms because they have legal problems. They hire law firms because they have personal problems that are being caused or exacerbated by a legal problem.

You now have an insight the vast majority of your fellow lawyers are utterly oblivious to. Now let's press this insight to even greater advantage for you, shall we? Here's how we can supermagnetize your marketing and give your small law firm an unfair advantage. Because as if speaking to the problem instead of the person weren't a big enough waste of money, the few law firms that even understand this concept still manage to get it all wrong.

At any given moment in time, let's say 20 percent of the people who may see a law firm's "*ATTENTION: You and anyone remotely like you*" marketing message even have the sort of problem your law firm is equipped to solve.

This means 80 percent of those marketing dollars is being wasted. What's more, of those 20 percent who do have the sort of problem your law firm is equipped to solve, it's a safe bet fewer than half are emotionally ready or willing to solve it.

So, while 80 percent of your so-called "competition" is busy going broke, marketing to problems instead of people, probably the next 19 percent is trying to market to everyone. And unless you have extremely deep pockets, you CAN'T market to everyone. You'll go broke marketing to everyone.

So, you have to discriminate.

It's not a bad word; in fact, it's your safe passage to prosperity and sanity.

Imagine going to trial as either plaintiff or defendant (it doesn't matter which for this example) and you get a do-over on your opening statement, a do-over on your direct examination, a do-over on your cross. Imagine if you could also get a do-over on your voir dire to eliminate any jurors you have second thoughts about, even during the trial. As if all that wouldn't be good enough, imagine if you also had the chance to interview the jurors privately, just before closing arguments. Would you take this advantage or leave it?

Well that's exactly the scale of the advantage your law firm can enjoy when most of your so-called competition is wasting 95 percent of their marketing dollars. And we'll be showing you exactly how to go about giving yourself this advantage before the end of this book.

But first let's put the enormity of the advantage you have before you into perspective. Because sometimes when we talk about how much the law firms grow when they begin to apply *Magnetic Marketing for Lawyers*, we're met with skepticism. Even though we have more case studies and testimonials than any sane person should have time to review. Seriously, it's a MOUNTAIN of proof.[5]

But as a lawyer, you already know people have a funny way of believing what they want to believe, even in the face of overwhelming evidence, until and unless your idea becomes their idea. So, let's see if we can transplant this idea of ours through these pages and get it planted firmly in your mind.

Suppose you and every other law firm owner in your market that's focused on solving a particular type of problem all got together and decided to "level the playing field." To make things "fair." And to do that, you each agree to spend no more than $1,000 a week ($50,000 a year) on marketing.

Except a third of everyone else wastes their $50,000 per year speaking to problems instead of people.

And a third of everyone else wastes their $50,000 per year speaking to everyone "because we don't want to discriminate."

And the last third waste their $50,000 per year by just shoveling it all into the waiting arms of marketing vendors who don't bother to

5 MagneticMarketingForLawyers.com/CaseStudies

pursue any sort of rational strategy and try to build a brand with lots of followers and likes and other vanity metrics that don't generate any actual income for those firms.

But thanks to the fact that you've read even just the first two chapters of this book, you now understand how to deploy your $1,000 per week so much more effectively simply by speaking to people, not problems. And not just "any" people, and certainly not "everyone." From now on your marketing is going to go narrow instead of going wide. It's going to discriminate by showing up in places where your target market is likely to be instead of trying to be everywhere. And it's going to discriminate by speaking only in terms that resonate strongly with your ideal target client, and we're not going to try and water down our messaging just to appease everyone else who is never going to hire your law firm anyway. This is called a "marketing strategy," and it will make you rich, but it may not make you popular with your peers.

A smart Magnetic Marketing strategy also cultivates future prospective new clients. It goes "upstream" from the point at which they're ready to make a decision and "brings them along." This way you have predictable cash flow for years to come. Don't worry; we'll get to this specific approach later in this book.

MISTAKE #3: SAYING THE WRONG THINGS

Not only does your marketing have to talk to the right person; it also has to say the right things to that person. When you say something that fails to connect with your target client, we call that a failed "Message to Market Match."

Going back to the example of Domino's USP, they understood their initial market perfectly—ravenously hungry college students desperate for something, anything, to ease the munchies. Their message was "fresh hot pizza in 30 minutes or less"—the perfect solution delivered to your doorstep in record time. THAT is a perfect "Message to Market Match."

What makes it even more powerful is that they entered the conversation going on inside their prospect's head—which in simple terms could be boiled down to "Hungry. Food. Now."

Had they instead focused on "delicious sauce, Mama's old country recipe, ingredients sourced from the finest, all organic farms, delivered in style by a man in a tuxedo ... " it would have tanked. Because that's NOT what the market was looking for, and it certainly didn't match the dialogue taking place in that college kid's mind as he was watching the TV or studying for finals.

Another key mistake many law firms make involves the language used in the marketing. When you focus on a specific group of people, you're able to tap into the vocabulary they use every day. Doing so is critical—for example, with musicians and magicians you would want to promise them "more gigs," not "more jobs." Golfers have a vernacular all their own as well, with "bunkers," "buried lies," "shanks," and "skulled shots," a.k.a. "wormburners."

Just as you wouldn't attempt to communicate with a Frenchman in Mandarin Chinese, you don't want to use "outsider" language and terminology when communicating a sales message to your prospective client.

You only know this when you truly know your WHO. You need to know more than just their demographics; you need to know their hopes, dreams, fears, and most importantly, the conversations that are going on in their heads, the things they will never tell you ... unless you ask.

MISTAKE #4: ASKING THEM TO DO THE WRONG THINGS

This boils down to asking for the sale too quickly without first narrowing down our universe of potential clients.

We live in an extremely skeptical age. Once respected professions and institutions now have practically zero credibility, including journalists, clergy, education providers, and so many more. And let us not forget that famous, oft-repeated misquote from William Shakespeare: *"The first thing we do, let's kill all the lawyers."*[6]

According to a Pew Research study in 2013 on professional public esteem, lawyers ranked near the bottom of the barrel. So when a potential new client who has never had any exposure to you or your firm or your values agrees to let you handle something as potentially involved as their estate plan, bankruptcy, divorce, or even just scheduling an appointment to discuss a simple speeding ticket, it demonstrates quite a big leap of faith.

Without first establishing a significant level of trust in your credibility, responsibility, and authority right from the get-go, you face a significant uphill battle enticing anyone to do anything, let alone sign on the line which is dotted.

Therefore, instead of going right for the sale out of the gate to everyone on the planet, a more effective marketing strategy is to first narrow down your focus by getting a subset of your potential market to qualify themselves by "raising their hand" in response to an offer that's much easier to say "yes" to—a free educational resource of some

---

6 Shakespeare's exact line, "The first thing we do, let's kill all the lawyers," was stated by Dick the Butcher in *Henry VI*, Part II, act IV, Scene II, Line 73. Dick the Butcher was a follower of the rebel Jack Cade, who thought that if he disturbed law and order, he could become king. Shakespeare meant it as a compliment to attorneys and judges who instill justice in society.

sort, possibly a webinar, a video, or a book. This enables you to begin that process of gathering a group of people who have a very specific problem that your firm can solve. It enables you to begin establishing credibility, authority, and trust, turning an unknown potential client into a self-acknowledged "lead" with whom you can follow up more intensely and personally.

We call this concept "lead generation," and we'll discuss it in much greater detail in just a bit.

MISTAKE #5: THINKING YOU CAN ADVERTISE ANYWHERE AND EVERYWHERE

Marketing used to be relatively simple when it came to choosing which media platform to use. CBS. NBC. ABC. PBS. Local radio. Local newspapers. Yellow Pages. A limited number of high-profile magazines. Billboards. And the few other outlying options of varying effectiveness, such as skywriting, smoke signals, and a strange new technology called "the World Wide Web."

As the giant reptiles vanished from our planet, so too has this once simple media menu. Today, you as a marketer face a far more complicated, diverse, and challenging array of options from which to choose. New media channels and technologies seem to appear daily.

This constantly changing media landscape challenges even the most tech-savvy marketer. Not only do you have to keep up with the latest and greatest, but you also face disruptions caused by shifting public opinion, government intervention, and even changes to corporate strategy. Google adjusts its search algorithms continuously, potentially rendering an easily found, SEO-optimized website practically invisible. In regard to pay-per-click (PPC) ads, whole businesses were destroyed when the infamous "Google Slap" completely shut down lead generation ads and systems that previously delivered handsome returns.

Because of this overwhelming complexity, many attorneys simply throw up their hands and outsource this task over to a so-called expert or ad salesman and then write the checks based on them saying, "You have to be on channel X." They mistake the choice of media for actually having a strategy.

The only way to avoid this mistake is to nail down exactly the WHO with whom you are seeking to establish a relationship. Once you know that, it's actually quite simple to choose which media channels to advertise in—you go where they go.

If they're on Facebook, you go on Facebook. If they read *Cowboys and Indians*, you advertise in *Cowboys and Indians* (and note—what you offer inside doesn't even have to relate in the slightest to the Old West; it just needs to appeal to the kind of person who reads that magazine).

And even though many consider them outdated, the Yellow Pages can still offer huge benefits if you're targeting an older demographic who continues to rely on their use.

You want to ONLY be where your WHO is and then you want to be EVERYWHERE they are.

It's a huge mistake to try to sort out all the different options for media without first having a plan for what you intend to use that media for. The worst thing you can do is make a series of random, disconnected marketing attempts across various media channels. Instead, you want to create a true system that attracts new clients in an organized way. Because it's only with this kind of system that you can achieve reliable, predictable results—so you know when you invest X, you will get Y in return.

MISTAKE #6: NO MARKETING SYSTEM

This is probably one of the biggest, most widespread mistakes made: marketing without a system.

Without a system, you are flying blind, literally throwing Jell-O against a wall, seeing if any of it sticks, and if, by happenstance, something does work, you have no way of leveraging that data because anything that did produce a positive result is now an oozing green puddle on the office floor.

Without a system, you're forced to pray for and then rely on one-hit wonders (e.g., remember the "Macarena"?) that offer you a brief moment in the sunshine of success but then vanish like dust in the wind. It worked, but you don't know why, you can't repeat the process, and once it's gone, it's gone.

This goes hand in hand with what we call "Rollercoaster Marketing"—where, when times get tough and clients are scarce, you throw everything plus the kitchen sink into your marketing efforts. If you're lucky and manage to catch a bit of traction, your funnel gets filled up and your firm's business successes start the ascent. So, you drop everything and get to work because your caseload's full and you're too busy to market and the inevitable perception is that you don't need to because everything's fat and happy. But this only delays the inevitable because when you stop marketing, your funnel will eventually dry up—new leads stop coming in, existing clients move on—so you start the descent, howling all the way to the bottom. And you're back to where you started.

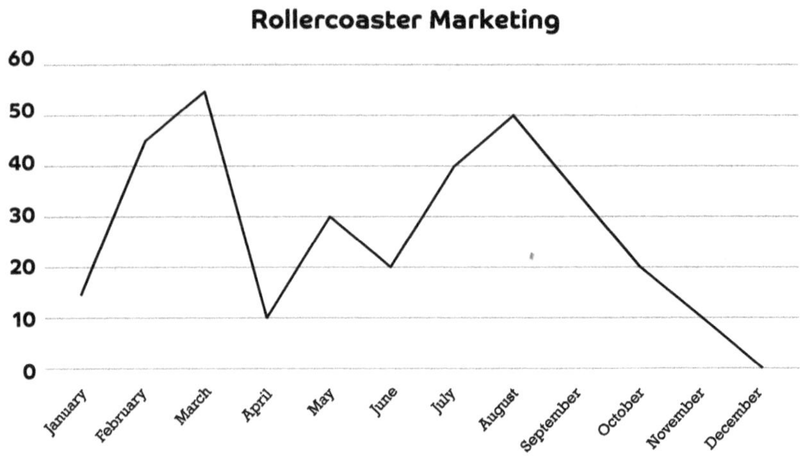

A reliable, scientific, predictable marketing system is what you must put in place instead. You want a system where marketing works like a faucet that you can turn on or off depending on the needs of your practice and where you want to go with it.

At a minimum, you want your Marketing System to focus on three key areas:

1. **Lead generation—The ongoing acquisition of leads for your firm**
2. **Conversion—Taking those leads and converting them into paying clients**
3. **Retention/referral—Keeping that client base intact and generating new leads based on referrals**

Once you have this system set up, you simply put it in motion and let 'er run. There are attorneys who have Magnetic Marketing systems that have been running essentially untouched for many years.

MISTAKE #7: CHASING CLIENTS

Almost as big a mistake as not having a system is the wrongheaded perception by attorneys of all stripes that it's your job to CHASE clients. While it may seem logical to do so, ponder the implications on a personal level for a moment …

Q: What's your natural impulse when you see someone following you in hot pursuit?

A: You skedaddle.

And that's what your prospective clients will do once they see you chasing after them—and no matter what kind of shape you're in, they can outrun and outlast you. You will wind up left in their dust … undoubtedly along with the rest of your competitors, because it's almost certain they don't know any better either.

Instead, consider a different approach. Stop chasing. Start attracting. Lay out something they would value as "bait" to magnetically attract them and that will cause them to take notice and request information from you. This "bait" could be as simple as a two-page report promising to solve a specific problem they face or a free video that answers some question that you know keeps them up at night. (You do this based on your research and how well you understand WHO your ideal clients are.)

This idea of having "them come to you" flips everything around and changes the game. Using this kind of approach, where you offer something of value for free in exchange for getting someone to step forward, raise his/her hand, and say, "I'm interested in learning more," gives you the opportunity to separate yourself from the competition, and it completely reverses the power position of who's chasing whom.

When you stop chasing, you no longer have to resort to gimmicks to set yourself apart from the school of hungry sharks circling at the mouth of the river waiting for clients to emerge into the ocean—your ideal clients are magnetically attracted to you, and it happens "upstream" from where all the gnashing of teeth is taking place with everyone else.

When you use attraction, this allows you to charge and collect premium fees. People pay more for a solution that they've already at least partially embraced, or better yet asked for.

Attraction brings to you clients who are more committed and likely to remain with you over the long term. Another benefit is that clients who come to you through attraction are naturally inclined to remain with you and continue to do business with you over and again.

Attraction also builds trust, which is a key to selling legal services in our exceedingly skeptical age. The client attraction system we recommend with *Magnetic Marketing* establishes your credibility and authority by delivering the results—initially on a small scale—exactly as promised, laying the foundation for an expanded relationship, bigger engagements, and greater trust as you continue to deliver real value.

Attraction brings to you clients who are more committed and likely to remain with you over the long term.

Attraction enables you to sell exactly what they want to buy because it ONLY draws in prospects who fit your criteria and mindset. You know them inside out, you know what they want, you attract them with something that you know works, and they'll buy and keep buying your services.

So, what kind of marketer do you want to be? Constantly chasing after people who may or may not want you? Or calmly waiting and watching as eager, new prospects knock on your door and ask for the help only you can provide?

MISTAKE #8: THINKING YOU HAVE THE AD BUDGET OF COCA-COLA

It's only natural to think the advertising you should emulate is what you see every day on TV. Because that's where the big ad dollars get spent—and by the biggest, most respected brands in business like GE, GM, Google, Apple, Microsoft, Kellogg's, Anheuser-Busch, and Coca-Cola.

Millions pour into the coffers of ad agencies to produce high-definition, high-dollar commercials for the itching eyeballs of the nation. With these ads, they hope to move us emotionally, to make us laugh, and to make us associate their brands with happy feelings so that when the time comes to make a relevant buying decision, we choose them.

That's the game they're playing. And the cost to join them at the table is enormous. Not even the biggest law firms on the AmLaw 100 have anything even remotely close to the ad budgets of these companies. In 2017 Coca-Cola's advertising expenses were $3.96 billion.

Do you really want to play that game too? You're not Coca-Cola. You're not going after every parched throat on the planet. You don't need to copy what they do in your advertising.

You need to do what works for you.

MISTAKE #9: THERE'S NO FOLLOW-UP

You undoubtedly see this all the time.

Let's say you and your spouse decide to go out to eat. Even though you always eat at a few tried and true establishments, you say, "What the heck, let's try someplace different."

So, you head into town and see a new restaurant has just opened up. It looks OK from the outside, the parking lot isn't full, but it isn't empty either, so you decide to give it a try.

You go in, get seated, and the waiter arrives and asks for drinks and then the order. Food arrives; it's actually better than expected. There's a nice dessert menu, followed by some coffee (equally good), and then the check, a tip, and out the door.

Overall, a relatively pleasant, enjoyable experience from start to finish.

That was your perception.

But you'll probably NEVER return.

Why? Because they didn't seem to even notice you existed.

Sure, all the basic functions of a restaurant were executed properly—waitstaff, food service, cooking, accounting, and so forth.

But they missed the ONE thing that could make or break their business.

They put zero effort into doing everything they could to make sure of your return.

There was no capture of name, address, even email.

There was no offer of a bounce back coupon to entice you to come back.

They didn't ask about your anniversary, birthdays, children, friends, none of that.

ZERO effort went into knowing you as anything but an ephemeral visitor out of the blue who showed up one night and then passed like a ship out to sea, never to be heard from or seen again.

Tragic.

> NOTE: At How to Manage a Small Law Firm, we recommend our members follow up regularly with clients with something we call a GAS Call—it literally stands for "give a shit," and the simple act of just doing that level of follow-up can make an incredible difference to your success.

THE ANSWER IS SIMPLE

When you truly know your WHO, you can magnetically attract all the clients your law firm can handle. And you don't have to do this by slashing your prices, chasing after everyone in hopes of catching someone, or spending yourself into oblivion trying to imitate the biggest firms in town with marketing budgets greater than your firm's whole gross revenue projections for next year!

You can't afford to make any of these mistakes, and you don't have to—because it's not about you; it's about them. Knowing them and their needs inside and out and then meeting them exactly where they live with just what they've been looking for.

Getting the right Message, via the right Media, to the right Market—it all starts with knowing your WHO.

CHAPTER 3

What Happens When You Attract Instead of Chase?

When you run a law firm, whether you're checking emails, looking at web-based appointment requests, or sitting in your office listening for the front desk phone, the worst feeling in the world is the same: Silence.

Without a constant flow of leads, clients, and cases coming in, your law firm is doomed to fail.

It doesn't matter how good you are, how motivated you are, how wonderful your skills and services are; none of that matters. The lifeblood of every law firm is LEADS and CLIENTS and CASES, and the beauty of *Magnetic Marketing* is that you don't have to suffer in silence any longer.

Instead, you allow your SYSTEM to magnetically attract potential new clients to your firm—prequalified, prescreened, already interested in you and what you have to offer.

And don't let the word "SYSTEM" scare you. What you'll discover in this book is simple to understand and straightforward to implement, even if you don't have any kind of technology background. In fact, lawyers have been using the "systems" described in this book for generations, long before the internet or email or social media, to build highly successful client-attracting machines.

It's all about NOT chasing clients anymore; it's about ATTRACTING them instead by:

- ➔ Abandoning strategies that everyone

else is using that just don't work

- ➔ Making the MARKETING of your law firm and its message the number-one priority of management
- ➔ Focusing your marketing on the needs and dreams of the clients you want to attract

The difference can be dramatic, as you'll see in these stories of lawyers like you who switched from marketing like everyone else and instead took that first step to implementing *Magnetic Marketing* principles for themselves.

"Went from Struggling to Massive Success with Lead Generation"

Ben Glass is a personal injury attorney who (over twenty years ago) had just left the comforts of a law firm to start his own practice. So, he did what seemed natural—Ben looked around at what other lawyers were doing, and he copied them. "If everyone else is doing it, then it must work" was the reasoning. But nothing seemed to make the phone ring.

Then one day Ben came across the original best-selling training ***Magnetic Marketing System and Toolkit*** (there wasn't a book like this at that time). The concept of lead generation marketing jumped out at him. He then understood that there was a simple process to get the right prospective clients interested in his business and a system for marketing directly to those people.

Ben didn't fully understand the power of Magnetic Marketing when he started; he just started following the system. But boy did it pay off!

Ben now has one of the most successful personal injury law firms in his area. He went from struggling to get clients to a predictable system that delivers clients on a daily basis. Today Ben is a father of nine, grandfather of two, an active soccer referee, and respected thought leader who continues to break the molds. Take a moment to think about this … Ben is the owner of a multimillion-dollar law firm that now helps far more people level the playing field with insurance companies versus the number of people his firm could help when he was struggling … and he still has time to live a great life! Systems.

"The Road to Success Is Paved in Pink"

Kristen Mark opened her private law practice, My Pink Lawyer, in 2008, catering to women and families for their estate planning, probate, and guardianship needs. Positioning her firm as a premier law firm for discerning women, Kristen's firm helps its clients avoid government interference, time delays, and family disputes down the road after the death of a loved one.

It wasn't an easy journey. In fact, after struggling for twenty-one years to succeed as a lawyer, Kristen quit her job to become a Mary Kay Director. It was a major step outside her comfort zone, providing valuable skills and confidence in herself. Becoming very successful in Mary Kay, she earned four free cars, including a pink Cadillac.

But Kristen became disenchanted as working evenings and weekends took their toll; plus, the net profits from the business weren't what she'd hoped. So, Kristen decided to return to law, opening her own practice, and named it—what else—My Pink Lawyer because of her connection to Mary Kay and the immediate recognition it gave her in the community.

In 2016 Kristen attended her first SuperConference, got to see Dan for the first time, and became hooked on Magnetic Marketing. She loved the stories from outside the legal profession and began thinking of ways to apply their strategies to her own law firm. She started implementing like crazy—mailing Shock & Awe packages and a print newsletter. She attended another SuperConference and implemented even more—including a livestreaming TV show on Facebook, creating evergreen webinars, increased use of videos on her website, and even writing a second book.

Kristen took the lesson to hone in on your IDEAL client to heart and discovered that even though all her marketing was geared toward women, she still had men—single men, widowers, and even divorced men—who were "magnetically" attracted to the principles upon which her law firm was (and is) built.

Other professionals in town called Kristen "stupid" for marketing to only "half the population." She says, "It's hilarious because their law firms haven't grown as fast as mine." She's also found that the people who are turned off by her marketing wouldn't be good clients for her anyway. This isn't sour grapes either. It's critical for you to embrace the fact that even if your firm can help "anyone," it can't help "everyone," and so you better get busy deciding who it's going to be geared for, or else you may find your firm isn't helping nearly enough people for you to achieve your own financial, personal, or professional goals.

Magnetic Marketing has enabled Kristen to practice law on her terms—from a northeast Florida office inside the building she owns, decorated exactly the way she wants, complete with a pink couch in the waiting room. With zero debt and a comfortable lifestyle she loves, she's now making more money with more time off than ever before.

"Nothing Moved the Needle until He Jumped Down the Rabbit Hole"

Francisco Sirvent started Keystone Law Firm in 2007 (under a different name) as a way to provide his family with a better life by helping other people with the big problems in their life—estate planning, asset protection, elder law, probate, and related litigation.

Their best clients are couples within two to three years of retirement who have a net worth of a million dollars. Usually, they come from white collar professions (teachers, engineers, lawyers, accountants).

Francisco started in 2007 with nothing—no book of business, no network, no referral sources. And worst of all, no one who had the answers. Other lawyers offered plenty of advice, "but it never seemed to create momentum."

The firm grossed between $80,000–$100,000 per year for the first four years, and Francisco was only able to support his growing family (wife and four young children at that time) by keeping overhead extremely low and penny-pinching everywhere possible.

Francisco attended networking meetings. Found introductions to financial advisors, hundreds of them, to build relationships. Used software to create automation and attended plenty of CLEs and bar functions.

Nothing helped. Nothing moved the needle.

The struggle cost him six years of his life. While his kids were cute and tiny, he was scrambling, working eighty-plus hours per week to be the attorney, receptionist, secretary, paralegal, and office manager. His wife got too little attention. They couldn't and didn't take the vacations they wanted, they couldn't save toward retirement, they accumulated debt—Francisco came to the brink of losing all hope of a better life.

Then Francisco received a copy of Dan's original book, *Magnetic Marketing*, when he engaged How to Manage a Small Law Firm to help him grow and manage his business. "I printed out Dan's rules of Direct Response and put them everywhere—my desk, my laptop, my phone." He decided to jump down the rabbit hole and started offering a free public seminar about estate planning. "That first seminar was the first time I'd ever set ten appointments in one day, and we haven't looked back since!"

Francisco was hooked from that point on.

The first year using this type of marketing was 2013/2014, and Francisco's firm grossed more than $200,000, more than doubling its best year before. And they've been growing every year since. In 2019 Keystone Law grossed $1.4 million and with help from RJon's team, the net was the highest it's ever been. By creating a better marketing system, Francisco's firm has been able to help fourteen times more clients than before, and that's enabled Francisco to build a custom dream house from scratch, propelled him to hire a professional firm administrator (COO) for the first time, and at last, the law firm is becoming less of a job and transforming into a business that isn't dependent on him.

Visit MagneticMarketingForLawyers.com/CaseStudies to see these and many, many, many more stories from lawyers who are students of *Magnetic Marketing for Lawyers*.

THE PROOF IS IN THE PUDDING

There are so many people running around these days touting the next big thing that it's become harder to know whom to listen to and whom to trust. Always another new kid in town.

As they say, the proof is in the pudding. And we want you

to know you can rely on *Magnetic Marketing for Lawyers* not only to help you build a better law firm and a better life today but also pretty much until human nature changes, which (sadly) we don't see happening anytime in the near future. Do you?

These stories represent just the tip of the iceberg of the lives changed—millions of clients every year who now feel empowered by the education-based marketing that's at the center of *Magnetic Marketing for Lawyers* and thereby find confidence to hire a law firm to help them have a better life, legal staff who can now look forward to stable and growing employment opportunities inside thriving law firms, the families of thousands of small law firm owners who have happier lawyers to share their lives with, and of course the law firm owners themselves liberated from a hamster wheel of a career.

Countless millions of lives have been improved because of the application of the timeless principles contained in this book, ever since the first version of the Magnetic Marketing System was released over twenty-five years ago.

Life is just different (better) when your firm makes the shift from "Chasing Clients" to "Attracting Clients." No matter when you are holding this book in your hands (or maybe technology has allowed it to be beamed directly into your brain by now), you can have confidence that the principles and strategies described in this book are reliable and timeless. And if you'll invest the time to build them, your very own Magnetic Marketing System (For Lawyers) will continue to serve you for years to come—attracting slam-dunk clients to your firm.

Even better news, with the ever-expanding number of media options now available and dirt-cheap technology that makes easy what used to be hard, it has never been more within reach for any solo or small law firm owner to put together a Magnetic Marketing System customized perfectly for YOU.

Note: Now you might be saying to yourself, *"But wait, my law firm is different ... what if I am in a commodity business? I HAVE to price my services lower than anyone else in order to get the business I need."*

First off, your firm is NOT different. Practicing law is NOT different. Every industry faces the same pressures to lower prices. Announcing yourself as the lowest-price option is both a cop-out and a recipe for disaster. Clients only resort to hiring a lawyer based on price when lawyers don't bother to give them a better way to make their choice.

If this is the route you choose to follow, we wish you the best. But understand, it's only a matter of time before someone else emerges to go after your clients with an even lower-priced option. Then you'll be forced to either lose those few clients you have or instead compete in a downward spiral to oblivion. It's a race very few can win and almost never for long. And the worst part about it is the clients who pay the real price because what they need is a strong and resourceful advocate, not a starving shell of a lawyer.

The beauty of *Magnetic Marketing* lies in the way it sets your firm apart from the so-called "competition" in a way that's focused on features and benefits you control—and that make your firm a unique solution for the challenges your perfect client faces. In essence, you eliminate price as the key component in the buying decision, and in reality most buyers of all goods and services, not just legal services, place price lower than other factors to be considered, such as convenience, quality, guarantee, and so much more, when given the chance.

Magnetic Marketing frees you from the danger of relying on pricing alone as your only or primary marketing tool.

CHAPTER 4

What This Actually Looks Like

The practice of the law is a profession—not a business or a skilled trade. *While the elements of gain and service are present in both, the difference between a business and a profession is essentially this: the chief end of a trade or business is personal gain; the chief end of a profession is public service ... to give peace and order to society. This is the function of the lawyer, his reason for existence—not primarily to make money or assist other men in their personal struggles or difficulties, but to give peace and order to society.*

—"A Profession Not a Skilled Trade," Judge John J. Parker, address delivered to the student body of the University of South Carolina Law School, Columbia, SC, November 30, 1955; as recorded 8 S. C. L. Q. 179; 1955–1956

This is the origin of the false premise that has undermined the success of solo and small law firm owners for decades: "Business or Profession?"

Never mind the misogynistic overtones or irreconcilable conflict between one of the core elements of the above address and the Oath of Attorney you took when you were sworn in to your state bar and your state bar's rules of professional conduct, which demand that you act as a zealous advocate for your clients, avoid all conflicts of interest, and help your clients in their personal struggles and difficulties. In other words, exactly the opposite of what His Honor suggests. This address also demands an impractical impossibility and reveals His Honor's entrepreneurial naivete and misunderstanding about what profit is and how it is created in a business.

You are here because you are willing to reconsider that entire paradigm. You are prepared to, or perhaps have already, rejected the false premise <u>Business or Profession</u>? Why can't it be both?

In point of fact, neither can long exist without the other.

The practice of law is a noble and worthwhile profession. And to remain independent in all practical ways, lawyers need the law firms they work for to be at least financially successful.

And for the business of a law firm to thrive, it must deliver quality legal services that meet or exceed reasonably set expectations of clients, and repeat business, and referral sources.

So, without the "profession," there is no business, and without the business, the "professional" looks a lot like a highly educated person who is sitting around with nothing to do. Thus the practical need for more leads and more clients exists for law firms of all shapes and sizes. Even nonprofits and government-funded legal offices have the same 7 Main Parts of a Successful Law Firm to manage and attend to. They just convert the "financial profit" into more services for their constituents.

We call these random and erratic acts of attempted marketing "STUPID."

Unfortunately, too many struggling lawyers insist on believing in (and hiding out behind) His Honor's fairytale belief about there being a practical way to separate the business and the profession. Countless struggling law firm owners have actually said out loud (whined like babies) when RJon has presented these practical realities of life, "I'm a lawyer, not a businessperson." To which RJon often wanted to reply, "Well, grow up, buttercup, because you became a business owner the day you hung out your own shingle!"

And so, there are countless struggling law firm owners looking for that fairytale magic wand solution that will solve all their marketing problems "for them." Search engine optimization, pay-per-click, social media, TV, billboards, radio, print ads, marketing videos that are totally devoid of strategy or a call to action. It all reminds us of the lines from that old song—"looking for love in all the wrong places"—the way most struggling law firm owners go on searching for someone to tell them what to do with their money.

We won't do that to you!

We are here to empower you to create your own marketing strategy and a system to make it work. Or at least empower you so you can recognize whether the person advising you how to deploy your marketing budget even knows what he or she is talking about. Most don't. Which is why …

The biggest mistake lawyers are allowed to make by their so-called marketing advisors is to immediately focus on the media without having a strategy in mind first or a system to implement the strategy once tested and proven to work.

Law firm owners are often sold media and pour money into redoing all their websites or making new videos, buying online traffic, or some other "magic wand" sort of thing that's supposed to be the Holy Grail of client acquisition.

We call these random and erratic acts of and disconnected investments in attempted marketing "STUPID."

You need to realize that most ad agencies and most media representatives have a great understanding and reliance upon what's called "Image" or "Institutional" advertising (a.k.a. "Goodyear Blimp Advertising").

When Goodyear flies a blimp over a stadium, they don't have any illusion that thirty-five thousand people are going to jump up out of their seats and run out and buy snow tires at halftime. They don't expect that to happen, and it's a good thing they don't because obviously it doesn't.

What they're hoping for and what they're buying into is the idea that over a long period of time, because these sports fans keep seeing the Goodyear Blimp over and over again, they will connect it with a happy and pleasant event (the game) and they will therefore have warm, nice, fuzzy feelings for Goodyear. And then, someday, when they have to go buy a tire, all of that comes together in their mind and causes them to buy a Goodyear tire instead of any of the alternative brands available.

That's incredibly high-risk marketing, and it seems there must be a straighter line to get from a person who needs tires to buying Goodyear tires than going through all of that rigamarole of building a blimp and hiring a pilot and finding a football game and flying a blimp over it.

There is, and it's called "Direct Marketing" or "Response-Driven Marketing" or—when integrated into a complete system of attracting and converting leads—*Magnetic Marketing.*

This approach is derived from what used to be called mail order.

The discipline of the entire mail-order industry—now the direct-marketing industry—is that for every dollar invested there is a direct, typically fast, and always measurable return of that dollar, plus, presumably, some profit. You can boil it down to two very basic ideas:

1. **Spend $1.00 on marketing, get back $2.00 or $20.00, fast, that can be accurately tracked back to the initial $1.00 invested.**
2. **Do NOT spend $1.00 on any marketing or advertising that does not directly and quickly bring back $2.00 or $20.00.**

Go back and reread these two steps. Make sure you fully grasp this life-changing principle. These two steps should inform EVERY action you take from this point forward when it comes to marketing your firm.

None of this is new, by the way. And it's almost certain that you've seen, heard, read examples of it on television, radio, in letters, and so forth for most, if not all, of your life. Maybe you have even participated in direct response marketing without knowing it.

Most media people and most ad agency people have little or no understanding of this kind of marketing. Most even fear "our" kind of advertising and marketing because it is so accountable.

To make this system work, however, the first thing you must understand in depth is WHO your ideal client is. Because even the best possible offer made to someone who is wholly unqualified or wholly disinterested is not going to work. It will fall on deaf ears.

Therefore, you've got to match your offers with precisely the right people.

KNOWING THE WHO IS THE MOST IMPORTANT THING YOU'LL DO

There's a story about legendary copywriter Gary Halbert, who once asked a room of aspiring writers, "Imagine you're opening a hamburger stand on the beach—what do you need most to succeed?" Answers included "secret sauce" and "great location" and "quality meat." Halbert replied, "You missed the most important thing—A STARVING CROWD."

Your job is to find that "starving crowd" who can't live without what it is you have to offer.

What we want to do in terms of targeting is to find good prospective clients for our firm who can be reached affordably, who are likely to want the legal services we provide, who are able to afford those services, and preferably who already know of us or are likely to trust us.

Once you get this down, and you nail exactly who your Slam-Dunk Client truly is—the person you absolutely want to serve over and again—then you'll be able to make your marketing "magnetic" because you'll be using words and phrases that'll attract your target audience. This makes your job much easier because you can talk to them using language they relate to about what it is they really want.

WHAT YOUR WHO REALLY WANTS

Knowing exactly what your perfect client wants is NOT as simple as it might seem. For example, there's the old story of the customer walking into the hardware store looking for a 3/4-inch drill bit. The mistake that's easily made is thinking the customer wants a 3/4-inch drill bit.

Wrong. The customer wants a 3/4-inch hole. The drill bit is just the hoop the customer is willing to jump through to get it. But to truly magnetize your firm to the client, you'd want to develop the habit of taking your thinking a step deeper.

Let's take it a step further than recognizing the "want" for a 3/4-inch hole ... what's the underlying need driving THAT desire? Is it simply to hang a picture? Or does our homeowner crave a lifestyle surrounded by elegance that makes their home the envy of family, friends, and coworkers? So, it's not just about merely needing a hole; it's about Pride and an increased sense of Self-Worth.

That's a much deeper longing, and tapping into THAT is where you want to connect with your WHO. You want to solve their REAL problem, not just sell them something.

It's very easy to get this wrong in your messaging.

For example, you'll see firms competing with one another offering "Estate Planning." Most adults who could benefit from an estate plan already know they should probably get around to getting their estate planned. It's not like the prospective new client goes into the estate-planning lawyer's office and that's where they first learn that they should probably get around to getting their estate planned.

The problem isn't that they're stupid and don't already know they should get an estate plan in place to protect their family, give themselves peace of mind, etc., etc.

The problem is all of the estate-planning lawyers are selling estate plans instead of selling the benefits of having an estate plan. Consider the following headlines:

> *"Looking for an Estate Plan that includes a will, a trust, and a durable power of attorney?"*

Versus this:

> *"Sleep Better at Night AND Feel Better About Yourself Knowing You've Done The Right Thing When You Let Our Firm Help You Plan Your Estate For Your Family's Protection."*

That's a much stronger, more emotional way of connecting to the prospective client using terms and phrasing that resonate with what's going on inside their heads. OK, let's try another practice area. We LITERALLY just did a Google search for "Criminal Defense Lawyer" and found four criminal defense firms whose websites could have been swapped with each other, and other than the names and numbers and colors, nobody would know because they all say almost the exact same thing:

> If you have been charged with any type of crime in Florida, contact the Law Office of NAME OF LAWYER, P.A. today. Backed by over FILL IN THE BLANK NUMBER OF years of experience, our criminal defense attorneys are intimately familiar with this complex area of law. Our legal team can help you make well-informed decisions about your future as we guide you every step of the way through the criminal process. Regardless of what type of charges you are facing or how serious they may be, we can help you resolve your situation. You can rely on us for the effective and individualized advocacy you deserve.

And they all talk about how "aggressive" and "tough" the lawyers are. And that pose. Arms crossed. Scowl. OK, we get it—you're tough and aggressive. But not one word about the person who is making the hiring decision or what the lawyers believe in or what the firm stands for. Versus this:

> You are not the crime you've been accused of. Your future does not have to get all screwed up just because you've been arrested. If you've been charged with a misdemeanor, please click HERE to learn how the process works and three things you should NEVER say to the police! If you've been charged with a felony, please click HERE to find out how to prevent things from going from bad to worse—much, much worse. And if you've been arrested but you don't know whether you're being charged with a misdemeanor or a felony, please click HERE to learn the difference and why it matters.

Which advertisement or marketing message do YOU think is going to work better? Why? Really, take a minute to think about it strategically.

Congratulations. You just invested probably a minute longer than the lawyers who are relying on the first website copy to feed their starving families.

Notice how generic the first ad is? Nothing compelling. Nothing about the human being whose life is being impacted by criminal charges.

No way for the prospective new client to reach out except for a phone number or a generic web form that offers no real value to the person who is sitting at home, alone and scared, quite possibly in the middle of the night.

C'mon, did any of the lawyers who wrote or settled for the first example even bother to think any of this stuff through? It's called "STRATEGY," and it's missing from most of the law firm marketing you'll ever see out there. Oh, and by the way, those two sets of copy have almost exactly the same word count.

In the legal industry, no matter what particular niche you serve, the number-one thing you're selling is a better future. Clients hire lawyers because they want the lawyer to help them create a better future for themselves or to avoid winding up with a worse future. When most people think about their future, they think in terms of three things: Their time. Their money. Their reputation.

> **In the legal industry, no matter what particular niche you serve, the number-one thing you're selling is a better future.**

How are your ideal clients using their time today versus how would most of your ideal clients prefer to be using their time? Maybe they're thinking about their time in terms of having more freedom or more peace of mind or less stress or more options, or having more time to spend with their children before they're out of the house.

How are your ideal clients earning or managing or protecting their money versus how would they prefer their relationship with money to be?

Reputation could be thought of by some types of clients in terms of their professional reputation or their personal reputation or the reputation they have with the person they see every morning in the bathroom mirror.

The more you know about how your ideal clients are making their living and living their lives today versus how they'd prefer to be living their lives tomorrow, and why it matters to them, the more pinpoint accuracy you can engineer into your marketing to maximize its magnetism to those ideal clients.

"But what about everyone else?"

What of them? If you could fill your firm's capacity with nothing but your ideal clients, would it really be so bad that your marketing message is irresistible to them but repels everyone else?

There's a lot to truly understanding your WHO, how they see the world, and what matters most to them. But the rewards are well worth it.[7] Having a solid understanding is only the first step, though. Now you need to connect what THEY want with what YOU have to offer. And it all takes shape with a simple triangle …

7 We hid this in the footnote on purpose to reward you for really paying attention. Here's how you find out how your ideal clients see the world and what matters most to them: you ask! Call some of your favorite former clients, and ask about how their life or business or career was before versus after you helped them.

CHAPTER 5

The Magnetic Marketing Triangle

Now let's get to building your Magnetic Marketing System. It has three big building blocks, each of which you can imagine as one side of a triangle:

- **Message**: A truly compelling, preferably irresistible, marketing message.
- **Market:** High-probability target marketing that identifies only those most likely to respond.
- **Media:** The most appropriate, effective combination of media used to deliver your message to your market.

These three can't be placed in any kind of sequential order because no single one is more important than the other and none of them functions very well without the others being in alignment. It is a closed triangle. Each feeds the others, and when they are made to work together, you will begin to feel the enormous power of a Magnetic Marketing System at work for you.

BUT you can render the triangle powerless if you get any of them wrong.

For example, you can deliver the right message to the right market, but if you use the wrong media, they will never get the message or have a chance to act on it.

Or if you get the media and market right but fall down when it comes to the message—then the right people will see or hear your message, but they may not be compelled to take action because you delivered the wrong message.

Finally, you could use any number of very popular media seen by millions of people and use that media to deliver a very compelling message, only the message isn't compelling to the market that media appeals to, and so your very effective media campaign will deliver a highly compelling message but to the wrong market.

You must get ALL three right.

MARKET

The previous chapter mentioned the need to find your "starving crowd." The idea of NOT going after every human who still has a pulse is probably a new concept for many attorneys, or at least they act that way. In fact, most of us have probably been guilty of the "throwing mud against the wall" (hoping something sticks) style of marketing at one time or another in our entrepreneurial career. Only some of us will learn from our mistakes, and others won't.

With *Magnetic Marketing*, we use a very different approach. Among other things, our approach is designed to eliminate waste to the greatest degree possible. Because every dollar or hour of waste you can eliminate is an extra dollar or an extra hour you can invest to tilt the marketing scales even more in favor of your law firm.

To eliminate waste, we must narrow our marketing focus to only the people most likely to want what we have to offer.

The basic way that most people choose their target market is **GEOGRAPHIC**. If you have one location, you may say your clients come from a thirty-mile radius. Some lawyers don't get any more sophisticated in targeting than that.

Targeting with only geographic information is like getting in a plane and dropping flyers hoping some of them hit the right people. That may be an exaggeration, but the truth is, with just some simple tweaks, you can make your geographic target marketing much more effective.

DEMOGRAPHIC information is about how old people are, how much money they have, whether they are married or single or liberal or conservative, what religion they are, and so forth.

That's another way to further define who your ideal client is—and you really should do this—but again, it's still only surface level. Geographic and demographic information are important, but to really magnetize your marketing, we'll want to go even deeper than that.

PSYCHOGRAPHICS delves deeper. It explains "why" people buy. It includes information like habits, hobbies, proven spending patterns, personal values, philosophical ideas about how the world ought to be and how they think about what they think about, even if they're not conscious of it.

Demographics and psychographics will allow you to create your ideal client profile—a detailed picture of people you would like to serve now and in the future. So how do you determine the psychographics of your target market? Here are some questions to ask yourself:

- ➔ What keeps them awake at night, staring at the ceiling, unable to fall asleep as it relates to the specific services you provide through your firm?
- ➔ What are they frustrated about?
- ➔ What is causing them pain, right now, as it relates to what you can offer?
- ➔ What is the single biggest problem that you can solve for them?
- ➔ What do they secretly, privately desire most?

> Demographics and psychographics will allow you to create your ideal client profile—a detailed picture of people you would like to serve now and in the future.

The last question is very important. For example, most people who sell marketing courses (ironically) only talk about making more money and getting more clients—they think THAT is the core desire for most people. But there's a deeper reason—for them and for everyone. No one really wants or needs more money. You can't eat, drink, wear, or use money itself as shelter. Each individual who desires more money has his or her own personal (very personal) reason, and after you've interviewed a few thousand people from all walks of life, you'll find that most of their real reasons—the ones they don't talk about in polite company—have little to do even with material possessions.

How do you determine your market's secret and private desires?

If you've been practicing law for a while and you've already carved out a niche, you can make some educated guesses based on years of experience. Just think about the time(s) when you've been able to deliver exactly what the clients have said they wanted and they're still unhappy—what was it you then realized they were really after? Another approach, if you've earned enough trust capital with your best clients, whom you'd love to be able to "clone," is to just ask them.

If you are just getting into a target market, one of the easiest things that you can do is go to online discussion groups and forums. Start reading what people are posting there and on social media. If you are really paying attention and read between the lines, you will be able to figure out what the real motivations are. You will be able to see what they secretly, privately desire most.

Immerse yourself in their world. If you serve a specific industry, read their trade magazines and go to their trade shows. Talk with them. Ask questions. Watch, listen, read what they say to their peers, how they talk about their lives, and what brings meaning and what causes pain. Do what you can to get inside their heads until their deepest needs and dreams become evident to you.

If you've been in their business, walked in their shoes, laughed and cried with them, then you'll begin to understand what they secretly, privately desire most.

And once you've done all this, you'll have a pretty good idea about your WHO. And then, of course, like any smart marketer does, you test it, refining as you go.

MESSAGE

The next building block, then, is the right message, as in:

> *What do you say to your marketplace, to your past, present, and future prospects and clients that is compelling, that is magnetic, that cannot be ignored, that must be responded to, that draws them to you like a bright porch light on a dark night draws moths?*

Do you have a great marketing message? Most law firms don't, and for sure most businesses don't. You put down the deposit on the space, move in some furniture, hang out your shingle, and then the message to the outside world is nothing more than "Hello! We're open for business." Oh yeah, we forgot, you sent out those announcement cards too.

A marketing message is a way of concisely and clearly saying to the right market, "Here's what we're all about, and here's why you should choose this firm."

So, you need to ask yourself, "What am I going to say to the marketplace, and why is what I say going to be interesting and appealing to the marketplace?" And don't be afraid to be polarizing. Polarizing is what we're after to protect your time, money, and energy from being squandered giving attention to the "wrong" clients who will never hire your firm—and even if they do, you'll wish they hadn't.

> **BONUS**: Visit HowToManage.com/MagneticManifesto to request a free copy of The How to Manage a Small Law Firm Manifesto, which is nothing if not polarizing and an excellent demonstration of this concept.

But in the beginning, your firm's message won't be as "developed" as RJon's Manifesto. Your message can be as simple as the firm's *Unique Selling Proposition*, which we talked about back in Chapter 1. Remember the example from Domino's Pizza, who built their empire based on this USP: "Fresh hot pizza delivered in 30 minutes or less, guaranteed"?

You can go out to the market with a USP like this and you'll almost certainly do far better than most of your competitors, who are probably relying on clichés stating "the best" or "number of years in practice" or something equally meaningless to the average client.

And seriously, don't let perfection get in the way of what's simply good enough. Good enough really is good enough. And with practice it will get better.

Now we'll take you a step deeper regarding promotional messaging—into the creation of special, highly appealing offers we call "*Widgets*."

WHAT'S A WIDGET?

We call these very special offers "*Widgets,*" and the best way to think of it is as an offer on steroids.

Let's say you provide business formation services. A common offer might be to set up a free consultation—a pretty standard sort of thing. In fact, there's really nothing about "free consultation" that screams "PAY ATTENTION TO ME!" because just about every other attorney in your area offers the exact same thing using the exact same language.

A ***widget***, however, ups the ante by tossing in extra elements to make it even more attractive, hard to resist, and impossible to compare against competitors. You can think of widgets as packages of services and bonuses and premiums and experiences bundled together, given a clever name, and promoted as a special, one-of-a-kind buying opportunity.

Widget-making is an important marketing skill. Once you've got it, you'll use it regularly and every day in your business via email, flyers, TV ads, newspapers, phone scripts for your intake department, speeches, and on and on. That's why it's so critical to understand the concept.

One of the best widget success stories comes from Las Vegas, in the hotel and casino business, where pretty much everybody offers the same thing, a place to come and lose a lot of money and have a good time doing it with a lot of lights and pretty girls. For decades that was the business in Las Vegas.

Years ago an amazing entrepreneur, Bob Stupak, took over the worst and last hotel on the Strip. He had to find a very different way to get people to come and stay at that hotel and gamble in that casino.

He didn't have a tremendous amount of money at the time to do advertising and marketing with, so the conventional ways that Las Vegas hotels market themselves was pretty much out for him.

Bob sat down, and he turned the hotel business and the casino business in Las Vegas into a very specific widget that he could hold up and people could see and get a grip on and understand and be attracted by and buy in advance of use.

Here's his widget. Ask yourself if you would respond to it, presuming you were convinced it was real.

> "Give me $396, and I'll give you two nights, three days in my hotel in one of the deluxe suites. There will be a bottle of champagne waiting for you when you arrive. You can have unlimited drinks the entire time you're here, whether you're gambling or not. Even if you're sitting in one of the lounges and enjoying the entertainment, you pay nothing more for your drinks. More importantly, for your $396, I'm going to give you 600 of my dollars to gamble with in my casino."

His widget included the room, it included the drinks, it included some extras like the champagne and souvenir dice and show tickets. It included $600 to gamble with while you were at his casino.

This widget turned that little hotel, which at the time that this started was on a Motel 6 level, into one of the largest and fastest-growing hotels on the Las Vegas Strip in its time, called Bob Stupak's Vegas World. It eventually became The Stratosphere.

Bob's "widget" proved so successful it afforded him the marketing budget to place full-page ads for this widget in *Parade*, in *Sports Illustrated*, in *Playboy*, in dozens and dozens of magazines and newspapers all across the country.

Bob filled his rooms by selling that widget, and that was really the business that he was in, the business of selling that widget. He didn't advertise any other type of accommodations. He didn't bother advertising his hotel as a hotel. He concentrated all his efforts and all his energy and all his resources on selling that widget.

These packages were prepaid. You buy your $396 package today, but you might not actually make reservations and go to the hotel until a month later, six months later, even a year later. In the interim Bob exchanged your $396 for a certificate, a piece of paper that entitled you to all the benefits described. He had your $396 in a bank account earning interest or funding construction and remodeling during the time it was not redeemed.

Plus, Bob knew his numbers. And he had a plan. Bob understood that a small percentage of customers who paid just $396 for their package would redeem it for two free nights in his hotel, a bottle of champagne, unlimited drinks, and $600 worth of casino chips. Bob's cost of goods sold for the free drinks, a bottle of champagne, and a room that would otherwise be empty was minimal (housekeeping and slight wear and tear). And we all know the odds of beating the house even with a $600 head start are slim. But how much do you want to bet every redeeming customer spent extra on food, entertainment, room upgrades, extending their visit, souvenirs, etc., etc.? And how about repeat customers who only "discovered" the property because of the widget and then told their friends? And that was all in the days before social media!

If you study this example closely, you see that two fairly mundane and ordinary businesses, the hotel business and the hotel casino business, were combined and turned into a totally different business. A different business was invented within the business, and that new and different business became the widget that was sold to the public.

Just think, if you were the owner of a hotel and casino, would you rather gamble on bringing in the occasional whale you could brag about to all your friends? Wouldn't it be a much safer bet to build a replicable widget where you know that when combined, your typical cost of goods sold and your average cost to acquire a customer are less than or even equal to the retail price of the widget? Systems are safer than heroics.

That's exactly the thinking process that you need to go through, so instead of creating an offer like "free consultation," which, again, is frankly pretty boring, what every other attorney on the planet offers, and is therefore easy to ignore, you need to capture attention by building on the formula that Stupak created long ago:

> **Here's what you get for only $Y, easily $X worth of value, including:**
>
> ➔ Feature—benefits—value
>
> ➔ Feature—benefits—value
>
> ➔ Feature—benefits—value
>
> ➔ Feature—benefits—value ... **and this one provides the means to follow up with them, so they'll likely buy way more than just $Y.**

For a business law firm, for example, you could translate this formula into something like this:

"Peace of Mind Corporate Formation & Education"

Congratulations! You're starting a new business venture and you're smart enough to know you should probably create a new corporation or a limited liability company to protect your assets and help shield you and your family from personal liability.

Our unique "Peace of Mind Corporate Formation & Education" program is just what you're looking for!

Priced at just $1,997 and backed by our 100 percent money-back guarantee, your "Peace of Mind Corporate Formation & Education" program comes with more than $6,599 worth of value that could save you TENS OF THOUSANDS later on down the road. Plus, countless headaches and embarrassment if you make any of The Seven Most Common Mistakes people make when setting up and managing their new corporation or LLC.

This "by demand" program sets you up for success and includes *all* of the following for YOUR complete peace of mind:

- Choice of Entity—Maybe a Corporation, or would a Limited Liability Company be best for your situation? And if a corporation, do your future plans require it be a "C" or an "S" corporation? Rest assured, we'll take the time to educate you and ask you all the right questions to help you make the right decision with confidence about which form of entity makes the most sense for your future plans. Changing entity types later on is time-consuming and expensive; better to make the right choice from the start—Value: $1,000.

- Entity Formation—This is the easy part. Once you know which type of company you want and why, then we'll handle the paperwork to get it all set up for you the right way, the first time. Because if you're starting a new business, the last thing you need to do is waste time on this simple administrative task—Value: $99.

- The Care and Feeding of Your New Entity—A big reason you're creating either a corporation or an LLC is probably to protect your assets and shield you from personal liability. But just because you've filed your papers with the Division of Corporations doesn't mean you're through yet. Don't worry—we'll make it simple for you because we're going to walk you through what you need to do step-by-step, from setting up your board of directors to required board meetings and your required annual reports so the state doesn't deactivate your corporation or LLC—Value: $2,000 (really, this is "priceless").

- The Trouble Always Begins with the Bank Account(s)—That's why we'll show you how to set up and manage the bank account(s) for your new business the right way, so you can save money on bookkeeping, protect your sanity, and protect your assets—at least part of the reason you're probably considering creating some sort of artificial entity is to avoid personal liability, so let's not blow it by messing up how you set up and later manage the bank accounts for your new business—Value: $1,500.
- The Right Way and the Wrong Way to Issue Shares—Corporations issue shares. Limited Liability Companies issue membership units. Regardless of which type of artificial entity you decide makes the most sense for your future plans, we'll guide you step-by-step through the process of issuing ownership units so you don't create problems for yourself that could be expensive to resolve in the future—Value: $1,000.
- An Annual Maintenance Plan, for added peace of mind, which includes:
    - **Vouchers for you to call us with questions at any time during the year** *[which is another way of saying, "opportunities for us to find*

more ways to generate more value and generate additional fees"].

- **Free updates for the following types of situations—XXX, YYY, and ZZZ** *[which is another way of saying, "opportunities for us to find more ways to generate more value and generate additional fees"].*
- **And an annual review to make sure your artificial entity remains up-to-date and current with your situation and wishes** *[which means we've got a sales call booked in a year].*

→ And by the way, we're going to throw in your first annual maintenance plan—valued at $1,000—for FREE!

Now that's hard to ignore, especially when presented to the right person at the right time with the right media.

Also, think about how this widget works strategically. Most lawyers make the mistake of trying to squeeze work out of every client right out of the gate. Instead, we think in terms of that client's potential Lifetime Value—so we're willing to start off small, working to get any piece of work and establish a quality relationship, so from that point forward we have the opportunity to earn a client for life.

By doing it the way shown in the "Annual Maintenance Plan" in the example above, you have one full year to show that client real value. Then, when it comes time for renewal, the client's positive experience with your firm has now made it a logical decision to stay with their annual maintenance plan—and now you have turned what could have been a single transaction into recurring revenue; you've now magnetized that client to you for life. Plus, you've overcome the "I know someone else who will do it cheaper" objection because unless they've read this book, chances are slim anyone else in your market is even *thinking* about any of this in the way you are now. And those who have stop themselves by putting up some of the most common objections, which are each easily turned inside out and can become big benefits for the ongoing management of a highly successful law firm.

Additionally, by selling your firm's services as a "widget" in this way, all throughout the year you're given more opportunities to discover more and more problems and provide solutions and even curate the client's consumption of other professional services. And since referrals out beget referrals in, this will further magnetize new business to your law firm from accountants, Realtors, insurance professionals, and of course from other lawyers, too, outside your firm's concentrated area of the law. Plus, now your firm will have a legitimate reason to be following up with all the clients who have bought the "widget" because they're on this annual maintenance plan—or just to conduct quality control calls!

CREATING IRRESISTIBLE OFFERS

Bob Stupak's "widget" created an empire for him because at the time it was irresistible.

With this widget, he managed to create a *Godfather*-level kind of offer—the kind of offer you simply cannot refuse.

Think about it. This offer, this deal, it just sounded too good to be true—room, champagne, unlimited booze, even $600 in gambling money (which had to be played at the casino; it couldn't be redeemed for cash). The total package just seemed amazing.

THAT is the kind of thinking you need to put into place when creating your offers. Too many lawyers come up with offers that involve zero imagination and barely move the needle.

An irresistible offer (again, think "widget" because that's what you'll be promoting) bundles together a variety of elements—price, bonuses, guarantee, speed, security, etc.—into something unique and compelling.

Frankly, if the widget you create doesn't cause you to pause and reflect to yourself, "Am I giving away the farm here?" for at least a moment, then the offer probably isn't good enough.

To be truly irresistible, it should literally overwhelm the client with value to the point that anyone who doesn't take action on your offer is someone you can have a high degree of confidence probably shouldn't.

For example, the first step many small law firm owners take to engage RJon's How to Manage a Small Law Firm is to schedule a free telephone appointment. If that goes well, they'll get an invitation to make a fully refundable "setup deposit" and attend a live "Discovery Day," where they are told they're going to get all their questions answered, have the chance to meet dozens of people from the How to Manage a Small Law Firm team, and ask them even more questions, and they'll get to meet hundreds of current clients—and even their spouses or significant others—whose growing law firms are managed by How to Manage a Small Law Firm. So, as you can see, for anyone who is even remotely serious about engaging and cooperating with a team of professionals to professionally manage the business of their law firm, this is a pretty irresistible offer.

But then RJon's firm takes it one step further just to bring it "over the top" and to protect themselves from ever having to wonder about "the one that got away."

If a law firm owner attends a Discovery Day, and for whatever reason decides not to engage How to Manage a Small Law Firm, they'll not only get a full refund of the setup fee that very same day, but they'll also get their travel costs reimbursed!

Can you just imagine how many thousands of hours of "chasing" something like this could save your own team? And not only the time but also the money and the energy that can be devoted instead to people who are much more serious, to giving them an even greater experience so your firm can earn them as a client for life!

Now none of this means you have to take a bath on the deals you make. Quite the opposite. Stupak watched his numbers, and he knew exactly what kind of ROI he got from every room key handed out. He also factored into the mix things like food, house winnings, return visits, referrals, and much more.

So, the widget didn't stand alone—it was just one piece of a much larger play he had going, involving his real business, which was to maximize the lifetime value of every client.

When creating your offer widgets in the *Magnetic Marketing System for Lawyers*, there are basically three types of offers.

- ➔ **Lead Generation Offers**
- ➔ **Consultation Offers**
- ➔ **Final Offers**

Each type of offer serves a specific purpose in building a positive relationship with your prospective client—establishing credibility and trust—all leading to the end goal of making the sale. Let's talk about each in a bit more detail.

LEAD GENERATION OFFERS

This is an offer whose only purpose is to, in effect, entice a prospect to raise their hand to identify themselves as having interest in a certain subject matter and to invite further communication. This last part is important because most states' bar rules provide very different guidelines for how a law firm may communicate with a prospective new client, depending on whether or not they've invited or given permission for further communication.

Often, although not always, the lead generation offer is free. You can find several examples of free "Lead Gen" offers scattered throughout this book. If for no other reason than to study how they work, we encourage you to take advantage of some of them!

You know how the minute you get a new car, suddenly you see that same make and model all over the place? Well, it's the same with lead gen marketing. You may not have given it much thought before, but now that you're aware that this kind of offer exists and of the strategies behind it, you will likely see them everywhere, except in almost any law firm's own marketing efforts.

For example, a law firm looking to represent employees who have experienced workplace-related injuries could advertise on their local cable television station using cheap "remnant" ad space to offer a "lead gen widget." A "remnant" spot is typically much shorter than a "regular" commercial, which is why it's usually very affordable. But it's going to be short, so you've got to have a solid strategy in mind to make it work. So, you could offer something as simple as a free information kit that promises to answer some of the most frequently asked questions a person is likely to have after being injured on the job, "Five Things NOT to Say to Anyone but Your Lawyer after You've Been Injured at Work." And since most remnant ads are going to run at night or at odd hours during the day—and since a person who has been injured at work is likely to be up at night watching TV or home during the day watching TV—there could be a good market media match. Everything is a test.

Once someone raises their hand and requests this "kit," we know this person is unlike almost everyone else on the planet at this moment and warrants special attention. They've obviously been injured on the job or knows someone who has been; why else would anyone be interested in this very specific information? Plus, now that they've "raised their hand" and given permission to be followed up with, as professionals we can take over responsibilities for the communication. After all, it's not their job to hire a lawyer.

Instead of using a strategy like this to provide an easy entry point, think about what most law firms do—they move straight to the sale! And remember, just because most law firms are doing it this way doesn't mean it's the most profitable way to run a law firm. In point of fact, most small law firm owners are sitting on top of an untapped gold mine of opportunities to grow their business. Even a "free consultation" may be—and obviously is, as evidenced by the great expense so many law firms incur to get anyone to take one—too high of a barrier to entry into a relationship with your law firm for many would-be great clients.

"Why?" you wonder … well, Arnold Taubman, one of America's most successful mall developers, coined the term "Threshold Resistance" in regard to the entrances to retail stores. It applies even more broadly to marketing.

Remember, your prospect doesn't want to pull out their credit card. They don't want to get off the couch. They don't want to even pick up their phone and punch in a number. At a mall it's hard enough to get them to enter a retail store where, God forbid, they face the very real possibility of some stranger walking up and trying to sell them something.

So, jumping right into "Sign up for a free consultation"—especially with a lawyer, regarding what is very likely to be an unpleasant situation—is a BIG threshold to get them to cross.

That's why starting with something that has a very low barrier to entry—like "call this number and get my free book"—is much easier to convert and provides a higher degree of response. There's far less perceived risk. So those interested are more likely to respond.

And by getting them to agree to that first step, albeit a tiny one, you increase the chances that further down the road, they'll become a client. This is a key to magnetically attracting clients. The addition of lead generation to your marketing system allows you to create a pool of ideal clients who have earned your special attention by taking the first, albeit tiny, step.

Therefore, since your firm almost certainly requires some sort of consultative-based sale (e.g., helping them think through where they are now versus where they want to be, why it matters, identify options, and helping them make an informed and empowered choice), it's wise to get the ball rolling with an appropriate lead generation offer of a free report that helps prequalify, preeducate, and precondition the right prospective clients who also have the right kinds of cases.

And just as importantly (and too often overlooked), your free report should help the wrong kinds of clients (or the right kinds of clients with the wrong kinds of cases) avoid wasting their time and yours by helping them make an informed decision NOT to come in for a consultation.

Remember, you have skepticism to overcome with almost every kind of sale, even for something relatively simple like defending a traffic ticket.

For example, if your firm files patents for inventors, you could offer a free report laying out "The 7 Mistakes Most Inventors Make When Filing Their Patent."

Better yet, consider how much more magnetic your free report would be if we took care to ensure a better message-to-market match by adding even MORE specificity with: "The 7 Mistakes Most Electrical Engineers Make When Filing Their Utility Patent."

> Pop Quiz: Which title do YOU like the best?
>
> The correct answer is: Your tastes are irrelevant. What you think doesn't matter. What matters is data. So, we conduct a split test and let the winner pay for your kid's college education.

CONSULTATION OFFERS

It's important to understand the lead generation offer, as it could very well be a foreign concept to you.

However, the consultation offer is probably extremely familiar and is likely the basic kind of offer you're making right now as an attorney.

The point of a consultation offer is to compel the prospect to make an appointment to meet—either face-to-face in person or over the phone or the internet—to discuss their specific situation as it relates to the services your firm can provide.

Again, do not underestimate how hard it can be to get someone—who may not know you—to drop everything and commit to this kind of meeting.

You can couch this in all kinds of friendly terms like "free" and "no obligation" and call it a "consultation," but everyone knows there's going to be a sales pitch in there somewhere. So, they have to make the affirmative decision to give you an hour in their day to find out IF you are everything you say you will be. They need to trade an hour that could be spent making dinner, meeting with a new client of their own, watching their child's soccer game, or even just the hour that they planned to spend reading a book—so let's not underestimate the "cost" you're asking your prospective new clients to incur so that they can meet with you for "free."

This is why you need to provide compelling copy that clearly explains the benefits (to them—not you) and articulates how easy and low impact this meeting will be.

It's important to make sure to talk about the transformation that will take place AFTER they finish the meeting with you. Here's where our earlier points about "emotional copywriting" come into play. You're painting a picture of how their life is lacking something now, but when they finish with you, all will be right with the world ... or at least better.

The most common objection most still-struggling law firm owners raise at this point is " ... but bar rules prohibit me from making guarantees ... " Respectfully, no, they don't. Bar rules do not issue a blanket restriction on lawyers offering any sort of guarantees, only on those making certain very specific guarantees related to the outcome of a case. RJon has been working with lawyers—tens of thousands of lawyers all across the country—since 1999, and he's had this same bounty outstanding and unclaimed for nearly a decade: "Show me any state bar rule that prohibits a lawyer from offering a money-back guarantee based on client satisfaction, happiness, or peace of mind, and I'll personally pay you one thousand dollars." So far, despite thousands of lawyers making thousands of excuses for not embracing these concepts (despite a mountain of evidence that they work), no one has made a claim on this bounty.

FINAL OFFER

Here's where you make the clear and direct call to ask for the sale.

In consultation-based selling, this could be done at the end of the consult (but it will work better if it's in the middle), or it could involve a short delay as you put together the specifics of the exact package of legal services you intend to provide.

It's important to note that the Final Offer is the ONLY model used by most businesses—they go right for the sale because they don't do any of the lead generation we've been talking about to set up the salesperson for success. And even worse, because the Final Offer Only mentality pervades their whole business and has them trapped on a hamster wheel, they also fail to follow up if their one and only offer isn't immediately accepted.

In the *Magnetic Marketing System*, you can go directly for the sale—and in some cases, it's the right thing to do. But it's absolutely not your only option. You can, instead, work your way through the sales process with multiple steps, starting with lead generation, moving on to consultation, and then finally closing the deal either at the consultation or via follow-up communications.

MEDIA

So, we've got a great message, and we've got a great market.

Here's the next challenge.

How do you take the message you so lovingly crafted and birthed and deliver it via the right MEDIA to these people you've carefully selected in a way that's effective, efficient, and affordable? How will it magnetically attract back to your law firm the perfect prospects who are ready, able, and eager to engage your firm—and only your firm—so you get to sell in a competitive vacuum?

It can be incredibly challenging, even for people who are technologically astute. The laundry list of media options available changes practically with every breath you take. And what worked yesterday may not work tomorrow. There's no possible way anyone could keep up.

So how do you choose?

Once you know your WHO, it's easy.

Where they live is where you target.

OK, it's likely that you've been told to be EVERYWHERE for EVERYBODY.

Instead, we're telling you to go everywhere your WHO actually is.

- ➔ If they're on Facebook (and Facebook has amazing capabilities to segment, divide, and conquer), then you go to Facebook.
- ➔ If they're subscribers to a highly focused, niche magazine that's eagerly awaited every month by a dedicated fan base, then you go there, and don't let the subject matter of the magazine discourage you. It doesn't have to be "on topic." It only has to be in the hands of your ideal target market.
- ➔ If they're hard-core conservatives who plan their day around talk radio, then you go there. If they're liberals who plan their day around talk radio on a different station, then you go there instead.

You do NOT go where they're NOT. It's not only not necessary, it's a waste of time, energy, and money. You go where they ARE instead. You can make a long list of media options that you can spend money on to deliver marketing messages. And these days, everyone is infatuated with the internet—and the systems that we teach work brilliantly online. But the internet is not a strategy. It is a medium, and it is not the only medium.

BONUS: Go to www.HowToManage.com/MagneticVIPDay to see a very special lesson about the difference between marketing tools and tactics versus what an actual marketing strategy is.

So, while going online is one option, another option is to use traditional print advertising. This could mean direct mail, freestanding inserts, Yellow Pages, or display ads in newspapers or local periodicals. You can even go on radio and television. On and on and on and on. In fact, it is precisely because everyone is so infatuated with the internet that there are so many great values to be had buying "old-fashioned" but still highly effective media advertising.

The reality is you should use a combination of all of the different media—a combination of online and offline.

Here are a couple of things you need to know.

First of all, all that stuff works, and it all can be made to work better with good direct-response methods.

But only a handful of all those things that you can do can be converted into a system. And SYSTEM is one of our favorite words. Systems means reliable, consistent, predictable results. Systems can be made to work for you. Systems have been managing the most successful businesses, not just the most successful law firms, for hundreds of years. You get a system working once, and then it keeps working on its own for a long, long, long, long, long time before you have to tweak it again.

You need marketing systems.

The next few chapters are going to lay out for you a marketing system that is so predictable, so reliable, so consistent, that when you have a system like this working for your law firm, you will know what it's like to go to bed knowing—not hoping, wishing, not even praying, but knowing—within a small, acceptable range of variance, what the revenues of your firm are likely to be twelve months from now. Because you'll go to bed knowing how many new files your team will be opening next month. Because you'll know how many prequalified and preconditioned prospective new clients will be scheduling appointments next week. Because you'll have a marketing system working for you. It's like a thermometer. You can even turn it up or down to get more or less any time of the week, month, or year that you want. It's that scientific.

But there are some rules you must follow …

CHAPTER 6
The 10 Foundational Rules

A good portion of Dan's book *The No B.S. Guide to Direct Marketing* lays out the ironclad rules that will transform any business into an infinitely more predictably powerful direct-marketing business. These also are the foundational rules that govern *Magnetic Marketing* ... even for lawyers!

Note that these are NOT "recommendations"—consider them mandates. Gospel. Etchings in stone brought down at great peril from the mountain. Please copy them down and post them anywhere and everywhere you work so they remain front and center of all marketing efforts you make from this day forward.[8] Use them to cut through the noise and manage anyone you hire to work on the marketing of your law firm for you. And if your whiz-bang marketing consultant doesn't know about these rules or proposes to spend your money on marketing that violates these rules, know that you're in trouble.

Resolve now that every ad you pay for, every email you send, every postcard or marketing letter you mail, every website you put up, everything and anything you do to market your firm and your services MUST adhere to these rules.

Yes, they are simplistic, dogmatic, and you will undoubtedly encounter specific situations where you find there truly is a rational reason to violate one or more. But if anyone ever proposes you spend your time, energy, or money on any sort of marketing that is violative

---

8 Download the 10 Rules of Direct-Response Marketing at MagneticMarketingForLawyers.com/10Rules

of any of these rules, they better be able to give you a rational explanation why.

But for now, sticking to these rules rigidly is the right approach. It's the best approach and the approach that will protect you from waste. You can experiment later, after you have gained practical experience in the use of these rules and have fully exorcised the demons of "brand advertising" from your mindset and from your law firm.

RULE #1—THERE WILL ALWAYS BE AN OFFER!

Number one, there will always be an offer, or offers. But generally speaking, just one offer at a time outperforms multiple offers that may distract the prospect and prevent us from building the strongest case possible for just one offer. On the internet especially, there's a popular idea that content is king. We would disagree. The sale is king.

All your marketing needs to have an offer telling your ideal prospects exactly what to do and why they want to do it right now. It should be irresistible and time-sensitive and give them some kind of transformative value if they take action. It doesn't have to get them from A to Z, but it ought to make a promise (and it better deliver on the promise) to get them at least from A to B, or even just headed in the right direction.

On the internet especially, there's a popular idea that content is king. We would disagree. The sale is king.

This should not be merely an implied offer like a store running ads saying, "We're here; come on in. Obviously, this thing is for sale." Yours should not be a generic offer like, "The Sale of the Century. This Weekend Only." Instead, wherever practicable, yours should be the sort of *Godfather* offer we discussed in the previous chapter—an offer so big, so bold, so perfectly targeted to the WHO you've identified as your ideal client that it is impossible for him or her to refuse. It could repel everyone else. But it should be irresistible to the "right" people.

This offer could be designed to generate a lead (with some sort of "lead generation magnet" like a free report, video, etc.) or to actually make the sale at that time. But an offer should always be made that gives the reader, viewer, listener, follower—recipient of the telepathic messages soon to be delivered by the next new technology that will come along, eventually—a way to improve his or her life even if only in some small way; otherwise we say it's a disrespectful waste of the prospect's time to look at your ad!

Needless to say, a great deal of thought needs to go into your offer, as we explained earlier. Regardless of the nature of the offer itself, the point is to make certain that every communication actually asks somebody to do something. Focusing on this injects a new level of discipline into all of your communications with prospects, clients, and the marketplace at large.

This rule should open your eyes to the sad reality that the vast majority of advertising presented is doomed to fail, or at best it dramatically underperforms what it's ad-spend could have otherwise produced for the owner(s) of the law firm, had there been thought of an actual strategy and an offer.

Here's an example of a free offer:

Visit http://www.howtomanage.com/MagneticVIPDay to see a recording of a segment from a VIP Day RJon hosted with a group of mostly seven-figure small law firm owners where he explains in response to a question they asked of him the difference between marketing tools and tactics versus an actual strategy. When you get to that page, see if you can spot the strategy at work and how we've made sure that just this one single free bonus should help you make your investment of time to study this book well worth it for you. That is if you're the sort of person who hates to waste time and money on marketing tactics or tools that don't work. If you are the sort of person who doesn't mind wasting your money on "feel good" marketing that impresses your friends and family but doesn't produce a measurable ROI, please visit LawyerFeelGoodMarketing.com instead. ← See, that's part of the strategy too! Attract AND repel.

RULE #2—THERE WILL BE A REASON TO RESPOND RIGHT NOW

The hidden costs and failures in all advertising and marketing are the "almost persuaded."

Your ideal A+ prospective new client with exactly the sort of problem or opportunity your firm is perfectly positioned to help them with saw your ad and was tempted to respond. They nearly responded. They got right up to the edge of response, but they set it aside to do it later or to mull it over or to check out other options. Maybe just at that moment, one of their children ran into the room demanding their attention or the phone rang or they remembered something their third grade teacher told them and that led them down a path that ultimately reconnected them with long-lost friends on social media but away from doing business with you!

When they get to that edge, we must reach across and drag them past it. There must be a good reason for them not to stop short or delay or ponder; there must be urgency.

Remember, hesitation and procrastination are among the most common of human behaviors. Your prospect doesn't want to move unless compelled to do so. Just like Homer Simpson, the last thing he wants is to put down the doughnut, get off the couch, and actually do something. Hence, you must provide a compelling reason to ACT NOW.

There are plenty of ways to add URGENCY:

- **Tie the offer to a hard-and-fast deadline.**
- **Restrict the offer to a limited number of clients.**
- **Remove incentives such as bundled services from the deal if they don't act right away.**
- **Add an extra bonus if they act before a given deadline.**

Those are just a few ideas; open your eyes to the world of experienced direct marketers out there, and we are confident you'll discover many more. Regardless, make sure to give a reason to ACT NOW.

"But I'm telling my story!"

Shared social values and a heartwarming story may be additive to the offer and make the prospective new client feel more comfortable taking action when called to do so, but your story alone, no matter how eloquently told, is not a call to action and creates no sense of urgency. Nor is humor a strategy, a call to action, or a reason to act now! Nor are all your undoubtedly impressive credentials.

The only thing that is a call to action is a call to action. And the only thing that is a reason to act now is a reason to act now.

Two final points on this subject:

First, you're the expert, not the client; so, let's not leave it up to the prospective new client, who has never navigated these unfamiliar waters, to understand the urgency of the situation he or she is in.

Second, if you could double the revenue of your law firm in the next eighteen to twenty-four months (yes, literally double) with not much more work, much more profit, and all while enjoying a lot more control over your time than you may enjoy today, how soon would you want that process to begin? Now you probably feel a sense of urgency. But you don't know exactly what to do, which brings us to …

RULE #3—YOU WILL GIVE CLEAR INSTRUCTIONS

Most people do a reasonably good job at following directions.

For the most part, they stop on red and go on green, stand in the lines they're told to stand in, fill out the forms they're given, and applaud when the applause sign comes on.

Most people are conditioned from infancy in every environment to do as they are told. Marketers' failures and disappointments often result from giving confusing directions—or no directions at all, so that their confused or uncertain prospects do nothing.

People rarely buy anything of consequence without being asked to. You must walk your prospect through the steps you want them to take in order to make the sale.

This is far more important than you might imagine. Take to heart the old rule: "A confused buyer—WON'T buy!" Anxiety rises any time you ask someone to do something from which they're unsure of what to expect or that they're unsure how to carry out.

Therefore, whenever you put together any kind of marketing tool, ad, email, sales letter, website, phone script, etc., make sure to examine it from the perspective of an unsuspecting client/prospect encountering it for the very first time.

Consumers like, are reassured by, and respond to clarity. Be sure your marketing provides clarity as a foreshadowing of what they can expect if they hire your law firm—and so they know step-by-step how to do exactly that!

RULE #4—THERE WILL BE TRACKING, MEASUREMENT, AND ACCOUNTABILITY

If you want real profits from your marketing, you are no longer going to permit any advertising, marketing, or selling investments to be made without direct and accurate tracking, measurement, and accountability.

Forget about likes, links, opens, shares, friends, followers, reach, visibility, views, or engagement—they can't be deposited in your bank account. All of that may be interesting, even indicative, but what matters is that for every dollar you spend, you can clearly identify how much comes back as a result.

This is for two reasons:

1. Business management by objectives is the only kind of management that works, even for law firms ... especially for law firms!
2. You need real, hard facts and data to make confident and intelligent marketing decisions. Lack of confidence leads to delay. Delay leads to lost opportunities. Especially in a professional services firm where the "inventory" is expiring by the minute.

If you loop back and connect this to Rule #1, you'll find an important key in tracking—offers. Different offers can be made in different media, to different lists, and at different times. You can include and assign promotion codes to letters, websites, order forms, phone numbers, and so forth. With this data, you can determine which offers and variations of offers work best for which lists and under what conditions.

Tough-minded management of marketing requires *knowing* things and then acting wisely upon what you know.

RULE #5—ONLY NO-COST BRAND-BUILDING

We are not opposed to brand-building.

We are opposed to paying for brand-building.

You can acquire all the brand power you need as a no-cost byproduct of profitable direct-response advertising and marketing as described in this book.

Our preferred strategy is simple: buy response, and gratefully accept brand-building as a bonus; NEVER buy brand-building and hope for response as a result. You're not in a popularity contest. You're in a profitability contest!

Paying for traditional brand-building may be fine, even essential, for giant companies with giant budgets engaged in a fierce combat over shelf space and consumer recognition. If you were Coors or Heinz or some other company like that, we'd say, feel free to play with the shareholders' money to buy name recognition. But if you're playing with your own marbles, beware because copying what the big companies do to build their brands can bankrupt you.

Even though held in high regard by media companies and advertising agencies alike, "brand" is not the Holy Grail magically able to cure all your business woes. Brand-building is best left to marketers with very deep pockets filled with other people's money. Your own fortunes are far better served by focusing on leads, clients, sales, and profits directly driven by your marketing system. There's that word again: SYSTEM. When the time comes to sell your law firm, which do you think the buyer (which would you) value more:

> We've invested millions to build the best-known and most highly respected brand-name law firm in town, and to keep it out there we're going to have to spend a few hundred thousand dollars a year from which we cannot reliably attribute any specific new business.

-or-

> Our marketing system requires one dollar of input to produce ten dollars of revenue to the firm, and we've been using it reliably to produce one million dollars of business every year for the last five years even though no one knows our name except our happy and appreciative clients and everyone they refer to the firm.

A brand is only a tool. It's not a panacea. Even the best brand must still be used, preferably as part of an overall marketing strategy, to generate new business.

RULE #6—THERE WILL BE FOLLOW-UP

People read your ad, get your letter, see your sign, find you online, etc.

They call or visit your website or place of business.

They ask your receptionist or your intake team some questions.

And sadly, in far too many cases, that's it.

There's not even the slightest attempt to capture the prospect's name, physical address, or email address. There's no offer to immediately send an information package, free report, etc.

This is a criminal waste of effort, money, and time.

When you fail to follow up, you are simply shrugging your shoulders and accepting waste as yet another cost of doing business. This is madness.

When you invest in advertising and marketing, you're not just paying for the clients you get. You are paying for each lead you generate, every call, every walk-in, every email, every reaction and response of any kind.

If an ad costs your firm $1,000 and that produces fifty calls, every call your team fails to follow up on is exactly like pulling a $20 bill from your wallet, taking a match to it, and watching it go up in flames. So, unless you truly do have money to burn, you need to make sure to follow up with every lead that comes through your door, be it a real door or a virtual one.

There are hundreds of variations for follow-up campaigns and strategies blending offline with online. Here are just a few ways you can follow up:

1. **Restate, Resell, and Extend the Same Offer**—Present what they didn't do or buy again in the best way possible. You can do this in a straightforward manner with letters or emails. You can also use "retargeting" online technology to keep the offer in front of someone long after they've seen it the first time—they'll see it on other websites they visit, their Facebook feed, and so on.

2. **Provide a Stern or Humorous "Second Notice" Tied to an Onrushing Deadline**—Present the offer again, reemphasizing the approaching deadline.
3. **"Third and Final Notice"**—Tie this communication to the deadline and the disappearance of the offer. Depending on practice area, it could be especially effective if this were to be delivered by snail mail, especially if the initial response was a request for "additional" information and your interpretation of your state's bar rules concludes that once a request for additional information has been made, "advertising rules" no longer apply.
4. **Change the Offer**—Sometimes you can change the offer relatively easily by swapping out a bonus from the original offer for something different.

Doing nothing with even one lead is like flushing money down the toilet. It is a serious lapse in judgment and waste of precious resources—YOUR RESOURCES—every time your team fails to follow up with every lead, every time.

"But I don't have anyone on staff to help me" ← And you probably won't, so long as you fail to maximize the ROI on every dollar spent on marketing!

RULE #7—THERE WILL BE STRONG COPY

The fact is, there is enormous, ever-growing, almost overwhelming competition for attention and interest—a daily tsunami of clutter that must be cut through or circumvented. In this environment, where literally tens of thousands of messages bombard your prospects every day, the ordinary and the normal are ignored, the cautious and calm messages unnoticed.

You already know you can't send a shy, timid, milquetoast person into a meeting to beg, in barely a whisper, for a few moments of the prospect's time. So, you can't do that with a postcard, letter, newsletter, email, web video, etc. either.

You want to send the Incredible Hulk instead—huge, glowing, neon green, stomping, impossible to ignore. He shows up, and the guy drops whatever he's been doing and pays attention. And this is doubly true if you yourself tend to be shy or timid. Let your marketing be your alter ego! It can't be a bait and switch, or else that will backfire. It can be an "enhanced" version of your normal daily demeanor.

> **You want to send the Incredible Hulk instead—huge, glowing, neon green, stomping, impossible to ignore. He shows up, and the guy drops whatever he's been doing and pays attention.**

But the copy can't just shout. Loud but irrelevant isn't much better than quiet yet relevant. Loud, you can grab attention, but you can't convert it to interest. The Incredible Hulk stomping into your office would get your attention, but he'd still have trouble bridging to interest and having you engage in a meaningful conversation.

Strong copy can be sensational and attention-commanding, but to be effective it must do so in a way that establishes relevance and credible authority. Here's a good example of a strong headline making a real benefit-oriented promise:

How to Get Divorced without Totally Screwing Up Your Kids, Alienating Your In-Laws, Becoming a Pariah to Your Friends, and Going Broke in the Process

Special report shares ten "do this, not that" mistakes that can save you tens of thousands of dollars in unnecessary legal fees

Most strong copy gets written backward, starting from the client's interests, desires, frustrations, fears, thoughts, feelings, and experiences (remember the emphasis earlier on nailing down the WHO?)—and then journeying forward to reveal a solution tied to your law firm.

By comparison, most ineffective law firm marketing copy takes the reverse path. It begins with the qualifications of the firm, the experience of its lawyers, and the area of law the firm focuses on. Rarely do you even see any law firm marketing copy that speaks directly to the client about what matters most to him or her in life, business, or career.

Most law firm marketing copy is firm-centric or centers on the law. The more effective approach is to focus your marketing copy on the client! Sadly, that's not what the majority of law firm owners or the advertising or marketing consultants they hire usually do. But their failure can be your great opportunity!

Here are two major mistakes your firm's marketing copy can't afford to make:

1. **Writing factually and "professionally" rather than emotionally**. Great copy communicates conversationally, one-on-one, just like you would sitting across the table from a friend you can't wait to let in on something wonderful you've just discovered or even something you're sincerely concerned about. And it makes no difference whether you're selling to *Fortune* 1000 CEOs or Al Bundy—your best approach is to write like you talk, speaking passionately, from the heart, with deeply emotional appeals.
2. **Being too "professional."** The Rules of Professional Conduct of most states require attorneys to be honest and candid and loyal to clients. They don't say anything about being boring. You can be professional and not boring. Just because every other lawyer writes to prospective new clients as if writing to a judge doesn't mean you can't write from the heart. And for that matter, there's no rule that says you can't inject some personality into your motions and briefs too! Many lawyers claim their marketing is boring and forgettable because of some fictional bar rules they can never actually cite. Others claim it's because their clients are smarter and more sophisticated than others

> **and therefore immune to sensationalism and hyperbole, perhaps even offended by it. Wrong. These beliefs are in contradiction to facts and experience. Instead, it has been our experience that most lawyers are simply afraid of the judgments and criticism of their peers, and so they'd rather stay broke but "fit in" than "stand out" and get rich. Good for them. Better for you!**

Look, we're not suggesting that any lawyer should be anything less than completely honest and forthright. In fact, we are suggesting you be VERY honest and VERY forthright in your marketing! Be honest about what your firm stands for, and be forthright about why you care. Don't be afraid to let your prospective new clients know that you are a human being who cares deeply about a cause or an area of the law or a category of client or something!

The fact you must embrace about strong sales copy is that you need it and you may have to learn to write it for yourself. If this concept happens to be brand new to you, start with our ***Magnetic Marketing System for Lawyers***® Toolkit available at MagneticMarketingForLawyers.com/System.

RULE #8—IT WILL LOOK LIKE MAIL-ORDER ADVERTISING

This rule is a great simplifier because it ends the tendency to try and emulate the majority of what you see most other lawyers doing with their advertising on TV, in magazines, in newspapers, online, etc. You are to go blind to anything except *pure* mail-order advertising. Anything else, shut the door, ignore.

We are specifically speaking of the formats, layout, and appearance of advertising—whether print ad or a webpage or any other item.

Here's exactly the right type of ad:

Classic mail-order ads are typically broken up into one-quarter or one-half of the page, give or take. The top quarter is for headline and subheads; the middle half for presentation of product or proposition, sometimes aided by testimonials; the bottom quarter for the offer and clear response instructions, often with a coupon.

The most frequently used alternative is the advertorial, which mimics an article.

The other reliable format is that of a letter, from you to the reader, at whatever length is necessary to do the job—sales letters can run four, eight, sixteen, twenty-four, even sixty-four pages!

And they can be repurposed—someone we both know literally tacked up a sixteen-page letter online as a website, drove traffic to it, and produced $1 million a year for nine years running.

To see real mail-order advertising, you need to assemble a diverse assortment of magazines in which highly successful mail-order companies consistently run full-page advertisements. These include *Reader's Digest Large Print Edition*, tabloids like the *National Enquirer*, and business publications like *Investor's Business Daily* and *Entrepreneur*. Also check out special interest magazines for model railroad hobbyists, gun enthusiasts, horse lovers, etc., as you'll find fractional and full-page mail-order ads.

Tear out and keep these ads as research; discard all others. Let these ads be your only models. If you respond to some, your mailbox will soon be full of direct mail that also follows classic formats and architecture. Open a file ahead of time and study what you get.

You'll eventually have a collection of advertisements that—if studied and used as a model—represents money in the bank.

If you're looking for a shortcut, we have compiled a few along the way, with templates and discussion about how to adapt some of the classic elements to comply with bar rules of most states. This valuable resource is available in our ***Magnetic Marketing System for Lawyers***® Toolkit (available at MagneticMarketingForLawyers.com/System).

RULE #9—RESULTS RULE. PERIOD.

Results rule. Period.

Do not let anyone confuse, bamboozle, or convince you that anything else is of any importance. Nobody's opinion counts—not even yours.

And there's no excuse for not assessing results anymore. With today's technology, it's easier than ever to link and track specific promotions to quantifiable results. You can even do what's called "split-testing" or "A/B" testing, where you match one headline against another to see which produces the best results and then continue the process over and again. Test. Monitor. Adjust. The goal is to gradually achieve the very best results possible.

The only thing that matters is the answer to the question "What results did it get?" When you implement this into your firm's culture, you change the way your firm communicates with its prospects and clients dramatically and forever.

> **NOTE:** A lot of what you have just read in the previous rules may seem weird, sound funny, or feel wrong to you. Too bold. Too aggressive. Too hype-y. Too unprofessional. Too far outside the box of what's deemed "correct" for lawyers. That's understandable. But it doesn't matter because, remember, your opinion NEVER COUNTS. You don't get a vote, and neither does your spouse, your mother, your golfing buddy, neighbor, your competitors, employees—nobody gets a vote. Not even us! The only vote that counts is the client's, and the only valid ballots are in the form of cash, checks, and credit cards.

RULE #10—YOU WILL BE A TOUGH-MINDED DISCIPLINARIAN AND PUT YOUR BUSINESS ON A STRICT DIRECT-MARKETING DIET

Many of the attorneys running their own firm who perennially struggle and suffer are very much aware of things that need doing but simply lack the will to do them.

Maybe it's a longtime vendor or employee or client, now a "friend," who you know is toxic and needs to be replaced, but you can't muster the will to fire them.

Maybe there's an ad that you keep spending money on that you know is failing to deliver results, but you lack the will to fix it or shut it down.

Maybe there's a website you know isn't producing either, but the very thought of getting it remade is painful, so it stays as is.

From this point forward, with ALL advertising and marketing, you have to be thick-skinned about criticism, tough-minded about money invested, extremely disciplined in thought and action, and dedicated to carrying out your game plan, all fueled by a resolute will to win.

IMPORTANT:

Anything that doesn't conform to the Ten Rules discussed in this chapter, do not let in at all. Just say no. And bar the door.

When you insist all ten of these Rules be respected by your staff and any vendors you hire to help you grow your law firm, you will cause a change—for the better—in the way your firm communicates with prospects and clients, dramatically and forever.

BUILDING YOUR MAGNETIC MARKETING SYSTEM

CHAPTER 7

Your Magnetic Attraction System

What's described over the next three chapters represents the foundational components of the complete Magnetic Marketing System for Lawyers®. We've never met a single attorney who couldn't take this foundation and apply it for use in their law firm. No matter the practice area. No matter the contours of the market. No matter the demographic of the ideal client.

We've met plenty who ignore what you're about to discover. Plenty more who had every good intention to implement it on their own but then lost momentum. Or got distracted. Usually by something that seemed pretty urgent at the time but that isn't all that important in the long run for the success of their business.

Meanwhile, there are thousands of law firms in practically every different area of the law you can imagine enjoying tremendous benefits from having done more than merely "intend to" implement what follows. Hopefully you have a good enough reason in your life to join the latter group.

When you put this system in place, you'll have a repeatable, reliable marketing machine working for you 24/7/365 to attract-convert-retain clients. No more guesswork. No more "feast or famine." No more random acts of marketing.

In this chapter we'll cover your ***Magnetic Attraction System***—built to attract prospects who fit your targeted WHO and get them to raise their hand, indicating that they have a problem your firm can solve.

It's important to remember when building this system that your business isn't just about YOU making a profit; it's also about the recognition that your clients are coming to you because they want to make a profit too.

Your clients are coming to you because right now they have a situation they don't want. It could be a situation where they're facing something bad that they don't want to suffer from anymore or in the future. It could be a situation that's potentially good, but they're frustrated because they don't know how to capitalize on it.

In any case, they have a situation they don't want to be in, and they're coming to your law firm because they're hoping to find a way to improve their situation.

It is CRITICAL that we truly understand this one fact if we are to produce marketing that is magnetic in its ability to attract the best clients to your firm. And so, without further ado, here's how The System works:

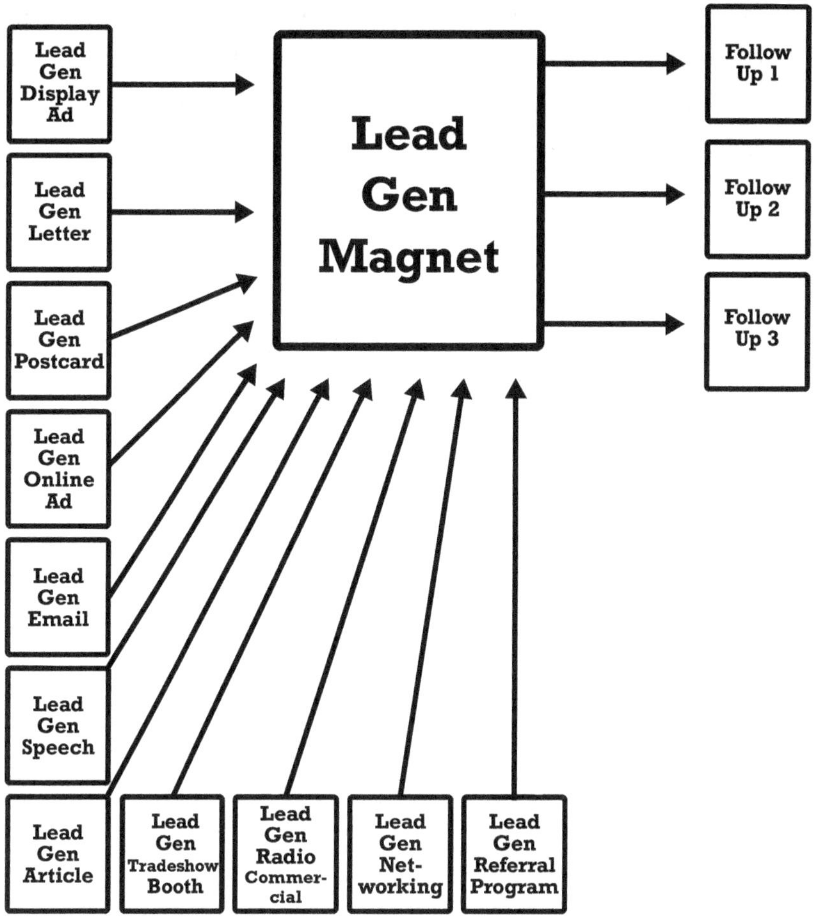

The Attraction System uses a variety of MEDIA channels where your target prospects hang out to let them know about your Lead Generation Magnet.

These media channels can include magazine ads, banner ads on websites, pay-per-click ads, emails sent to lists they've subscribed to, direct mail, business cards you hand out when meeting someone, display ads in newspapers, and so on. Don't get too distracted by the media. Its only purpose is to present your Lead Generation Magnet.

The Lead Generation Magnet is the special "Widget" you are offering to get individuals—from the greater population of prospects—to distinguish themselves from the rest by indicating a special interest in your narrowly tailored Lead Generation Magnet. For example, a single person who has never been married and has no children probably isn't going to feel compelled to take action if they're reading a magazine and see a Lead Generation Magnet entitled "How to Tell Your Teenagers That You're Going to Be Getting Divorced." Good! Because that person isn't the ideal target client for a family law firm that caters to the unique concerns of parents with children still living at home. But if you're a parent with teenagers still living at home and you're beginning to realize that you're probably going to be getting divorced, then this Lead Generation Magnet is probably pretty compelling.

The whole point of the Lead Generation Magnet is to give the right prospective new clients a way to self-identify and thereby transform themselves from a prospect into a "LEAD" who warrants special attention. And more importantly, a lead who has given you permission to follow up with them. Your Lead Gen Magnet can be offered for sale or for free, and we've seen a wide range of different price points work when used strategically.

Once a lead raises their hand, indicating they have a problem or an opportunity, and gives you permission, you are now permitted—arguably, you even have the professional responsibility—to follow up with them regarding the information they requested.

Everyone who raises their hand gets put into a "bucket" or database or list from which you then follow up with messaging aimed at either converting them from a Lead to a paying Client or disqualifying them as a Lead so you can invest maximum time and energy into building a relationship with everyone else.

This approach transforms your advertising from a "hope but can't tell if it works" model to a "know if it works" system. Now you're investing in reaching out directly to people you KNOW you can help and who have indicated they have a problem your firm can solve. You can run the numbers based on the results you're getting from your lead generation ads—calculate to see that for every $1 you invest you get $2–$10 or more back. This is a huge improvement over Goodyear Blimp type of advertising, where there's no way to accurately measure and you have no idea whether the ads have any effect at all.

CREATING YOUR LEAD GENERATION REPORT/GUIDE/MAGNET

The best Lead Generation Magnets contain information that has real value to the prospect.

It can be simple, brief, delivered via offline or online media, and crafted to attract exactly the prospect or client you want.

It can be a free report or a checklist or even a cheat sheet on a subject of prime interest to your preferred client. Remember, it doesn't matter if it's of absolutely zero interest to everyone else, so long as it's irresistible for your ideal clients.

The purpose of all of these is to position you and/or your firm as THE reliable, knowledgeable, and approachable authority in your field.

Your Lead Generation Magnet has four main jobs:

- ➔ First, to generate and enhance response to advertising.
- ➔ Second, to reinforce and strengthen the prospect's unhappiness with their current circumstances and problems that your firm can provide the solution to.

- **Third, to establish both your authority and empathy.**
- **Fourth, to position the situation so that the prospect is predisposed to accept your recommendations favorably and set the stage for them to want to work with your team, not just you.**

In many cases, the free report is nothing more or less than a disguised persuasive long copy sales letter. But keep in mind, the best and most persuasive sales letters are actually quite informative; they help answer a lot of frequently asked questions and provide much clarity.

A lot of lawyers hire inexperienced copywriters, though, who feel the need to be stingy with solutions to a prospective client's problems. You don't need to do that. Remember, we're looking to establish a long-term relationship, not a transactional one. So, it's best to include legitimately valuable information that solves a real problem. It doesn't have to solve all the problems. But it should at least help the prospect solve one problem, even if it's just the problem of being overwhelmed and confused.

When your firm's marketing promises and delivers real value, the prospect will see that you are a good source for answers and be more open when you suggest logical next step(s).

A lot of people balk at giving away valuable information, but that way of thinking is backward. Plus, it's not like you have a shortage of valuable information, do you? And besides all of that, information isn't what the client is ultimately after. They're after results, and to get results, they need help to put the information you'll share for free to practical use. We all understand that the information alone isn't enough, but it's the first step, and it's a smart first step for most clients to take, so why not make it an easy step for them by providing a ton of valuable information that demonstrates what your firm is all about?

When your firm's marketing promises and delivers real value, the prospect will see that you are a good source for answers and be more open when you suggest logical next step(s).

On the other hand, if you're stingy with your information and don't reveal anything of value in your Lead Gen Magnet, the prospect will assume (probably accurately) that there's no value in exploring a deeper relationship with your firm, either.

Here are a couple examples of information-based Lead Generation Magnets:

➔ ***"The Seven Things Every Struggling Restaurant Owner Needs to Know Before Declaring Bankruptcy"***—This report could describe key resources/strategies to help a restaurant owner facing major challenges, which may involve ways to conserve cash, practical tips for negotiating with creditors, ideas for how to avoid spooking staff, and so forth. Obviously, one of the seven things would include making an appointment to discuss the different debt relief options available. And what about all the non-restaurant owners? Well, this particular Lead Gen Magnet, which will appear in media that caters to restaurateurs, might not be as "magnetic" to them. So what? We can easily create a separate Lead Gen Magnet entitled ***"The Seven Things Every Struggling ~~Restaurant~~ Shoe Store Owner Needs to Know Before Declaring Bankruptcy"*** and place a separate ad in media that appeals to shoe store owners instead.

- ➔ Offering a free book, ***The Top Ten Things to Know If You Have Been Injured in a Car Accident in STATE***—This resource lays out the risks involved with speaking with police without an attorney present, things to say/not say when contacting insurance, what you need to record with photos after an accident, and of course, why having an attorney is critical to making sure you're protected.

When creating your Lead Magnet, here are a few important writing tips.

Avoid "me, me, me, we, we, we" speak.

Some Lead Generation Magnets talk too much about the firm or, worse, about the lawyer, and not enough about the prospect. The prospect does not care about you or your business per se, only about the wonderful things that will happen for him as a result of working with your firm. Translate every fact and feature listed in your report into a benefit for the prospect. Be client-oriented, not lawyer-oriented. Use all the data you gathered about your WHO and talk to them in their language and about their real problems.

Don't overeducate.

You want to inform and impress, but not tell everything you know. The client doesn't need to know everything. They didn't sign up for law school. They just need to know what they need to know to make sense of their situation or to help themselves make things better in some way, shape, or form.

Tell people what to do, what to expect, how the process works, how to think and how to avoid thinking about their situation, and what the possibilities are (both good and bad), but not necessarily how to do it all themselves. Most people don't really want to do it all themselves. Use your Lead Gen Magnet to simplify the situation a bit, to show them a better way to approach things and avoid the wrong ways, to help them gain clarity and make progress on their journey. Your free or even paid Lead Gen Magnet doesn't have to solve all their problems in life. It just needs to help make their life better in some real way. In fact, one of the best responses you can get from your Lead Generation Magnet is "Now that I have a better understanding of my problem or opportunity, can you help me resolve it?"

Don't forget the call to action.

If you don't have a call to action (CTA), you've wasted your time and money. To paraphrase Zig Ziglar, "Is your free report a sales professional, or a professional visitor?"

Tell the prospect exactly what to do, when, why, and what will happen once he or she takes the action being suggested. It's helpful to offer an immediate gratification incentive for that requested action, such as a special bonus or perhaps special payment terms. The CTA could be a number of things, depending on how complex your sales funnel needs to be.

- ➔ You could go directly for the sale by including pricing, features, bonuses, guarantee, even a deadline.
- ➔ You could instead offer a ticket to a workshop or some type of appointment-based consultation, with an invitation to schedule a telephone call or web or face-to-face meeting.
- ➔ Or you could send them to a website or some other additional information resource (visit HowToManage.com/MagneticAppointment to see an excellent example of this).

Create and use powerful titles.

The title of your Lead Generation Magnet is very important. Like a headline, it has to interest people enough to want it and then motivate them to consume it when they get it.

Take the time to create a powerful title. Where do you get great titles? Model the attention-getting headlines you can find on supermarket tabloids like *The Enquirer* and on the covers of magazines like *Cosmopolitan*, *Reader's Digest*, and others.

These headlines have to sell those magazines off the rack. Of course, the subject matter probably won't directly apply to legal services, but the structures of these headlines will.

MAKING THE LEAD GEN OFFER

Making the offer for the Lead Generation Magnet involves two steps:

Step 1: Sell the prospect on getting the Lead Generation Magnet.

Step 2: Collect contact information for use in follow-up.

(After you finish Step 2, you deliver the Lead Generation Magnet, which leads right into the Conversion System, discussed in the next chapter.)

Let's talk about Step 1, which involves making a strong sales pitch to convince the right kinds of clients to request your Lead Generation Magnet.

Do NOT underestimate the difficulty of giving something away for free. People are reluctant to share contact information, especially given the amount of unwanted SPAM they suspect will come their way, as well as privacy concerns related to sensitive legal issues.

So, you need to make the case for why your Lead Generation Magnet will solve a specific problem, heal a burning pain point, address a real heartfelt concern they're dealing with, etc.

Your options for presenting your offer of a Lead Generation Magnet are many and varied:

- ➔ Business card
- ➔ Postcard
- ➔ Phone script
- ➔ Website
- ➔ Facebook/YouTube/social media
- ➔ Banner ad
- ➔ TV or radio commercial
- ➔ Email
- ➔ Speaking

You can (and should) offer your Lead Generation Magnet anywhere and everywhere.

If you do so in person, it's easy—just get the prospect's business card or contact info. Then send the Lead Generation Magnet to them. Over the phone, just write down their contact information. While this may sound old-school, it remains quite effective, especially when dealing with target markets that skew older, to offer your prospective new clients a twenty-four-hour recorded message and have them leave their info there.

One of the most productive lead generation ad campaigns on radio nationwide instructs listeners to call a voice mail number and leave their email address. Then the marketer sends a free report, which has a sexy, exciting title and promise of interest to his target market.

Don't miss that point—your Lead Generation Magnet needs to sound sexy, exciting, informative, the magic pill to cure whatever ails you. The ad copy used to promote it likewise has to frame its benefits and value with powerful, emotional language. The Lead Generation Magnet offers transformation, pure and simple, and anyone would be a fool not to take advantage of it—and now.

One of the primary mechanisms today for collecting contact information is online with a dedicated, simple webpage called a landing page or squeeze page.

You probably already have a big, fat, catchall site that has a mountain of content on it.

If you're going to do lead generation, you should not send prospects into that. Instead, send them to a very simple landing page.

You may have noticed all the different landing pages we've been sharing with you throughout this book. As you may have guessed, each is "keyed" to a different offer that is tied to a different follow-up system. And depending which one(s) interest(ed) you enough to respond, the technology we use will apply a different "tag" to your contact information so we can zero in on what you're most likely to respond to when we follow up with you later!

In the interest of full disclosure, both of us are practically Luddites and do not know how to program any of this technology. Neither do you! But while we're on the subject, beware those who know how to operate the tools but don't have any strategies.

The landing page or squeeze page is very, very simple. In fact, the simpler the better. Because the main thing you want them to do is to give you their contact information in exchange for your Lead Generation Magnet. So that's the main thing you want to show them.

This page doesn't include any kind of navigation options or a menu bar with "Home," "About," etc. Nothing to distract the prospect who is trying to raise his or her hand from doing the main thing you want them to do when they get to this landing page, which is keyed to an offer and tied to a very specific follow-up campaign.

You're not trying to build a brand. Not trying to entertain or inform. You're not trying to get likes with this page. All you are trying to do, and the only thing worth measuring with this page, is to discern whether and what percentage of the people who do show up actually give you their contact information and permission to follow up with them. Don't let anyone tell you anything different. This is the one and only goal of your landing page.

Once you have a person's information, you send them your Lead Generation Magnet and then put them into your Magnetic Conversion System.

IT'S ALL ABOUT MAGNETIC ATTRACTION

This chapter should make 100 percent clear what we mean by Magnetically Attracting leads as opposed to chasing them.

Yes, you lay out the offer of a Lead Generation Magnet—the free report, the information kit, webinar, checklist, etc.—to as many of your WHOs as possible. But it's not chasing; it's simply laying it out there to see if anyone's interested enough to step out of the pack and raise their hand.

By doing so, you've enticed the sort of people who are interested in your very strategically targeted Lead Generation Magnet to take that very first step on their own. They've crossed the first threshold barrier. It's a tiny step to be sure, but it's an important one. They've said YES for the first time about something you have to offer; you know who they are and can now begin adding momentum to their journey with a Magnetic Conversion System.

CHAPTER 8

Your Magnetic Conversion System

Now that you have managed to get your ideal prospect to raise their hand, it's time to fire up your Magnetic Conversion System—the goal of which is to turn them from someone merely "interested" into an enthusiastic paying client.

The diagram below shows the different elements of the Conversion System:

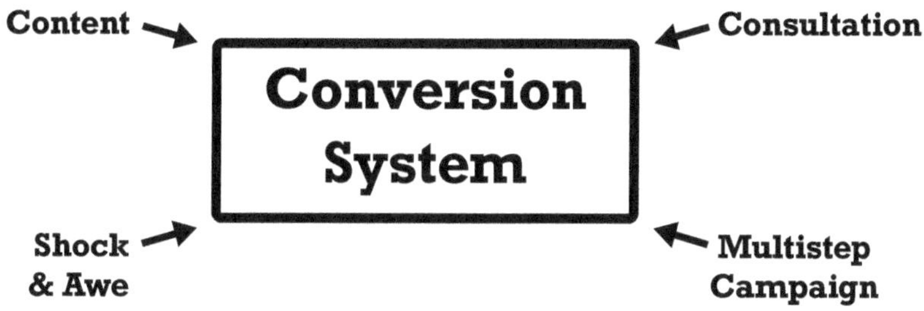

Please note that we could have arranged these as a flowchart, but that could have given you the impression that there's one way this "must" or even "should" happen. Instead, these components can be mixed and matched and sequenced in different ways. And once you begin to experience the power of an effective Magnetic Conversion System for your own law firm, you'll no doubt find endless enjoyment measuring and analyzing, then tweaking and testing, different ways to arrange these components to maximize results.

Always measuring and analyzing. Always tweaking and testing. Anyone who tells you they have the one and only way to do this is either a fool or a liar. The good news is, once you start thinking of marketing this way—as one big series of tests—it's liberating! There's really no way to go wrong unless you stop. Or worse, never get started. So, let's get started today!

That's right, the key is to implement SOMETHING. If you're reading this book on an airplane or somewhere it's not practical to get started, you can still get started, even if only in some small way. Take out your calendar, and carve out half a day every month for the next three months. In just ninety days, you can begin to experience the benefits we've been describing in this book and that thousands of other law firm owners enjoy every day. Better yet, visit MagneticMarketingForLawyers.com/System, and we'll make it virtually impossible for you to ignore the commitment we're asking you to make to YOURSELF.

> **Always measuring and analyzing. Always tweaking and testing. Anyone who tells you they have the one and only way to do this is either a fool or a liar.**

DON'T LAWYER THIS TO DEATH!

Unfortunately, as we mentioned earlier, law school drills into far too many attorneys a formula for total entrepreneurial failure.

"Never ask a question (in front of a jury) you don't already know the answer to" … soon becomes "Never ask a question (anywhere) you don't already know the answer to" … soon becomes a culture of "Don't try anything new unless you already know exactly how it's going to turn out."

But that's not how winning gets done in the real world of business. The winners in business ask lots of questions we don't know the answer to yet. Then we test. And we learn. And we get better.

And our businesses grow. One lesson learned at a time. Pretty messy, isn't it? Nothing like the pristine halls of The Ivory Tower.

This is why you see so many law firms that are totally stuck. Being run by lawyers who are afraid to look silly, to stand out, to be different. So, they stay stuck just so they can fit in with everyone else.

Hopefully some of the ideas you've been exposed to in this book already will prevent you from letting your law firm become one of the lemmings. They'll stand around at a bar function complaining about all the money they're wasting on marketing and that they don't have enough clients and that the clients they have aren't the right clients. Meanwhile, they're paying for unused inventory (staff capacity) and rent, chasing every new "easy button" marketing doohickey and shoveling untold amounts of time and energy into trying to find new clients and new leads—yet are unwilling to follow up with prospects they already have in order to maximize the investments already made. It boggles the mind.

Indeed, this should inspire YOU—because putting a Conversion System in place in your firm will literally create an unfair advantage over your so-called "competition," who almost certainly won't do anything anywhere close to, or as detailed as, or as systematic as, what you can do just by following the principles already learned in this book. And now one more … all the components of the follow-up lead conversion system are based on one overriding principle:

"Show Up Like No One Else"

We're about to tell you something that most of the law firm owners in your market are completely oblivious to: the biggest competitor that your law firm faces isn't any of the other law firms in your market; it's every other marketer in the world who is vying for your client's attention.

So, while everyone else is showing up looking like and sounding like everyone else—and worse, talking about the same things everyone else is talking about (themselves)—you can show up like no one else.

Sure, everyone else will probably criticize you.

But the right kinds of clients whom your message has been carefully calibrated for will be attracted to your law firm like none other.

Therefore, your goal in your Conversion System is to show up like nobody else. Stick out like a sore thumb among the tens of thousands of sales messages that are bombarding your prospects every day. Because your marketing message is competing for the attention of the client with everyone else who is competing for the attention of the client—not just other law firms.

> "Am I going to give my attention right now to this problem that calls for the services of a lawyer, or this other problem that requires a plumber?"
>
> "Am I going to give my attention right now to my kids, or am I going to watch my favorite show on television to escape all these problems (or even opportunities) that are vying for my attention?"

When you judge your firm's marketing by the milquetoast marketing of other lawyers, you completely miss the point. You're ALL losing out to the marketers who are willing to stand out.

You stand out by standing up for something or standing against something that the client cares about.

It's important to understand that the higher up the income ladder you go, the more often you'll find lawyers who are being paid more for *who they are* and/or *what their law firm stands for*—and not just the technical aspects of the legal services provided.

What most law firms do can easily be turned into a commodity. That's why LegalZoom presents such an existential threat to most lawyers. But who you are and what your law firm stands for is unique—there's only one, and therefore the value is established accordingly. Showing up like no one else reinforces this fact.

Let's talk about a few ways to do just that.

MULTISTEP CAMPAIGN

Most law firm marketing is not very sophisticated at all—and you'll note that since we're competing for the attention of our clients against everyone else, we're not going to make the mistake of limiting our analysis just to what other law firms are doing. Especially since most law firms are doing almost everything wrong.

Here's what it looks like when you analyze what most marketers (not just law firms) are doing: Print up a brochure. A lot of them. Put them in a burlap sack. Rent a plane. Fly low. Shake sack. Hope.

We can do better.

What we want to do is identify a small, carefully selected, manageable target market and set out to become the dominant presence in that target market in as short a period of time as possible.

Why small? Because the quickest way to having more profitable marketing is to dominate a market, and all things being equal, it's quicker to dominate a smaller market than a larger one. So, the biggest marketing mistakes most lawyers make is not thinking small enough. We'll ask, "Whom is your service for?" And they'll answer, "Everyone." And we'll say, "If your service is for 'everyone,' then what you are really telling everyone is that it's for no one in particular." And we'll get blank stares.

Show up for "someone" and they'll love you for it. Show up

trying to appeal to "everyone" and no one is going to get very excited at all about anything you have to offer. If everyone's a priority, no one's a priority.

In terms of a geographic target, we'll ask, "What's your target market?" "Miami." "Well, if we had a magic wand and we could somehow get everyone who needs a lawyer in Miami to hire you, what would actually happen to your law firm?" The answer is, you'd soon go out of business and likely lose your bar license in the process for all the bar complaints that would follow due to your law firm being so completely overwhelmed!

Any way you slice it, demonstrating the entrepreneurial maturity to focus on one target market … or one target market at a time … is the most profitable way to go.

And now let's consider the practical limitation of targeting "Miami." Let's suppose we're going to design the world's best sales piece—could be a direct mail letter or a postcard or a website or a billboard on the side of the road—regardless of the media type or tools, let's just say for the purpose of this example that it's the best.

But even the best marketing piece isn't going to work to maximum advantage if we only put it in front of the prospect once. Just imagine the following scenario playing itself out in a thousand households occupied by a thousand of your ideal prospects:

<u>Prospect Thinks to Himself</u>: "I'm a father of two young children. I'm married, we own our home, and our total household income is $85,000. I really need help with this legal problem. I sure do wish I knew a lawyer who could help me make sense of my specific type of situation."

<u>Your Marketing Piece Shows Up</u>: "If you're a father of two young children, married, and own the home you live in with a total household income of $85,000 and you're having this specific type of

problem and it's affecting you like so, then here's what you can do right now to begin making things better today."

You'd have to agree that's about as good as it gets, right?

Except it's 3:00 a.m. when the message arrives. Or it's 7:00 a.m. and the prospect has to get his kids off to school. Or it's 2:00 p.m. and just as our prospect is about to take action, his boss walks past his desk, so he shifts his attention back to work. Now it's 6:00 p.m. and he's on his way home but he doesn't have the letter with him, or he can't find the website on his phone while stopped at a red light. Now it's 7:00 p.m. and it's time to help the kids with homework and get them ready for bed. Now it's 10:00 p.m. and he just wants to put up his feet and relax for a little while to take his mind off his troubles.

And there you have it, folks; our most excellent marketing piece has STRUCK OUT.

Not because there's anything wrong with the message or the market chosen or the media used to deliver it. We nailed it on all three counts.

It got up to bat all right but then struck out because it only got the chance to swing at one pitch, not three.

No matter what your marketing budget, it will be put to more effective use if we shrink the size of your target market to allow more points of contact with fewer people, rather than fewer points of contact with as many people as your last marketing dollar will afford.[9]

The point is to have a BIG impact with "someone," not just a small impact with "everyone." And here's the secret to accomplishing

---

9 Caveat Emptor: Most marketing agencies get paid to produce a marketing piece and then a percentage of what you spend to promote or send that marketing piece, regardless of results. They earn the same amount sending one piece to twice as many people as two sequential pieces to half as many people. Same fee to them either way, but the sequential approach requires more effort on their part.

just that: if you want impact and you want response, then you must have repetition. The two are inextricably linked.

But you can't afford to do repetition the way Madison Avenue wants you to—by spending huge dollars on the same ads that show up again and again where EVERYONE can see them, hoping that someday it will be the right day for that one in a million and your ideal client will respond, finally. That's not the answer.

The answer is a series of targeted and sequential communications—they could be letters, they could be emails, they could be postcards, they could be a blend—that take place over a short period of time, each one reiterating your offer and call to action. Each communication building upon the last to make the case for taking action on your offer.

Think about how you win over a jury:

1. **You begin making your case during voir dire (market selection);**
2. **You lay out your message in the opening statement (initial offer);**
3. **You build your case, coming at key points again and again, each time from a different angle with each different witness (multistep campaign);**
4. **And then, at the end, you give the jury a clear call to action so they know exactly what you want them to do, why it's important (to themselves), and how to do the right thing (call to action). Except, when it comes to marketing, the jury gets to award us the verdict at any time during the trial, not just at the end. And if**

we're smart about our choice of media, market selection and the message we show up with, the jury doesn't even have to listen to the other side. Your unfair advantage, indeed!

A series of repetitive, related communications delivered strategically and systematically wins trials, and it wins new business too.

There's magic in the multistep structure.

These communications are typically fifteen days apart, although you don't have to adhere to that timing exactly. In some practice areas where there's real urgency (criminal defense, for example), testing will likely cause you to compress the cadence of the communications.

Regardless of the timing, each successive step ought to clearly refer to the previous one(s). We call that linkage. Just like a conversation. Or the chapters in a book. We wrote this chapter based on the expectation that you read the previous chapters of this book, with each successive communication making the case a little stronger as this goes along. And you can afford to make a stronger argument with each successive communication because of the foundation and the rapport that's been built up.

"But what if they didn't see my previous communication(s)?"

Flip back through the chapters of this book. Consider how the best trial lawyers handle trials that stretch on for days or weeks. Think about how successful negotiations are conducted over extended periods of time. We always provide a fresh recap of the main points, but we advance the point with each step. We don't just keep making the same point again and again and again like most marketers do. And keep in mind, if the prospective new client is seeing the now stronger messaging, it's because they're still engaged, so you must be doing something right!

In a perfect world, your follow-up sequence would never stop. But in reality, the first one you build will probably only have three steps.

Then, with testing, it may grow to five steps, and then eventually (until testing shows us the point of diminishing returns) your firm's marketing sequence will be built out to last forever. And don't you worry; we'll be sure to send out an alert if and when either of us ever achieves that laudable goal of perfection.

In the meantime, let's just focus on your first three-step campaign.

Step 1. Opens the case with your opening statement and a call to action.

Step 2. Continues the conversation where the first step left off, usually because it had to be brought to a logical conclusion and includes a call to action. Don't believe anyone who tells you it must "fit" into an arbitrary number of pages or minutes.

Step 3. Continues the conversation, summarizes the argument(s) that came before and "ups the ante"—this is your last hurrah. This is your closing argument. It's your last chance to make an impassioned plea to the jury/prospect to do the right thing. This is NOT the time to be subtle!

ADDING MORE CREDIBILITY WITH CONTENT

A simple three-step sequence works great for most practice areas. Certainly better than those sad little two-step sequences some people settle for. But there are times when you need to extend the sales timeline to further establish your authority and the credibility of the firm. In cases like these, you probably want to consider bolstering your positioning by following up on the initial Lead Generation Magnet with additional, related content.

For example, the initial Lead Generation Magnet might be a

video training, which is then followed up by a series of additional videos on that same topic. Just resist the temptation to turn this into a law school course. Your prospective new clients don't need to know—likely don't want to know—everything there is to know about your area of expertise. They only need to know—probably only want to know—enough to make an educated decision about whether, when, why, and where to get help to solve their problem.

But you don't have to limit yourself to videos. You can follow up with any number of things, such as emails, reports, online assessments, even books, ESPECIALLY if it's a book you have written—if you could use help in making that book a reality, reach out to the team at AdvantageFamily.com.

When doing this kind of extended campaign, it's typical to hold off asking for the sale up until the very end. Until then, you just continue providing valuable insights, and each new piece of content ends with a "stay tuned for coming attractions" message. The basic approach looks like this:

Identify a problem and offer a solution that begets the next problem for which you offer the next solution and little by little, solution by solution, you earn trust by delivering real value while everyone else is just screaming, "Nice to meet you; now hire me!" For example, it's very likely your mind is now open to the possibilities and you can see and maybe even smell or taste what kind of amazing life you could be enjoying if only you had a Magnetic Marketing System working in your law firm. Now you have a new problem. How are you going to live with yourself if you don't get around to implementing a Magnetic Marketing System in your law firm? And so now you are likely far more open—relieved even—to know we have another solution for you. Go to MagneticMarketingForLawyers.com/Blueprint to get a complimentary blueprint you can print out, tape up on your wall, and follow the steps yourself. Of course, if you've been paying attention, you already know that complimentary blueprint will indeed clarify and simplify and show you how to do all of this on your own if you want to. And it will also share with you a way to dramatically shortcut the process and get you to the money much quicker ;-).

The final piece of content is where you would make your real call to action, laying out all the critical elements of your offer, features, benefits, pricing, guarantee, etc.

BLOWING THEM AWAY WITH "SHOCK & AWE"

A related idea is to bundle a bunch of high value content items into a single package and then deliver them all at once in what's been called a "Shock & Awe" package.

The name is derived from the 1992 Gulf War, when US forces overwhelmed Saddam Hussein's military with overwhelming force. The objective with your marketing "Shock & Awe" is likewise to overwhelm the prospect with evidence that you are indeed head and shoulders above any other competitor ... and that he cannot (should not) attempt to handle his case on his own.

Your Shock & Awe package could include anything as long as it delivers real value. It can help the prospective new client make sense of his or her situation, evaluate options, gain confidence that there is indeed hope, feel better knowing they're not alone and that others have been through something similar, understand the steps involved, etc. If your Shock & Awe package is just filled with junk, then that's the impression your prospective new clients will have about the rest of what their experience with your law firm is likely to be like. As we've said before, don't be stingy. Here are some examples of things you could include in your very generous Shock & Awe package:

- Consumer report guide(s): Reports written by your firm to position it as the expert in a given area of the law.
- Printed Special Report(s), audio and/or video of interviews, guest appearances, podcasts, presentations, etc.—ideally these should provide practical steps a person can take to help himself/herself solve their own problem. (Oh, what's that, you say? Now that you understand this isn't quite as simple as you imagined, you're more open to getting some help? What a smart choice!)
- Letters to the editor of various publications written by members of your firm that demonstrate the values, philosophies, and the point of view of your law firm.
- Newsletters: Back copies of your monthly newsletter.
- Articles or press releases: Anything you have written or that has been written about you.
- Self-Assessment and Score Analysis Tool.
- Testimonials: Anything and everything anyone has ever said about your firm, showing overwhelming proof that your firm is the only choice they should be going with.

- ➔ Case studies: Typically, a former client recounting their own experience step-by-step through the process so that your prospects can have hope that if someone else made it through this process, they can too.
- ➔ Lead Generation Book (again, authored by you is best).
- ➔ And don't limit your thinking to just serious "information"—you can include cookies, candy, toys, T-shirts, and so on—as long as it's RELEVANT.

One estate-planning law firm we know of sent us a box with a teacup that had Grumpy from Disney on it, some teabags, a bag of cookies, along with a DVD and a note about enjoying a nice cup of tea and cookies while you watch this video so you will feel less grumpy whenever you think about protecting your family.

Now THAT made an impact. That is how you show up like nobody else.[10]

You'll definitely want to include at least some item with your **Call To Action**, which could lead to either a direct sale or to an in-person meeting.

---

10 We know what you're thinking, "A DVD? What is this—1999 all over again?" Well, guess what? This $7-million-dollar estate planning firm caters to an age group demographic that still has DVD players—and for those who don't, the label of the DVD includes a link and a password to see the same video online.

WRITING COPY TO SELL WHEN FOLLOWING UP IS ACTUALLY VERY SIMPLE

Here's how to write copy that sells like a rock star, and it's really, really simple.

Are you ready?

Charles Dickens has already written the best book on selling like a rock star that's ever been written. You've already read it. Studied it. Wrote essays about it. Maybe even performed it in the school play. You've all seen the movies and the adaptations of the movies and the derivations of the movies.

The book: *A Christmas Carol.*

Now, when most lawyers write sales copy, they write copy that sounds like the Ghost of Christmas Past—telling the client all of the things they've already messed up.

That never works.

Instead, you want to write copy and sell like the Ghost of Christmas Future—helping the clients see what's coming if they DO versus what's coming if they DON'T change their ways.

That's it.

You can sell millions of dollars of services, products, experiences, anything if you just sell like the Ghost of Christmas Future—by having the courage to care enough about your prospective new client, to help them see what's coming if they do versus if they don't change their trajectory.

But that's not the way most lawyers would prefer to do it. The way most lawyers would prefer to do it is to cite all kinds of precedents, explain the law, hide behind rules and regulations.

But that's not where the client finds the urgency to make the decisions they need to make in order to do something about their future. And unless you can invent a time machine, bring them back to the past to fix the mistake they've already made, and undo it, there ain't nothing you can do to change that, and rubbing their nose in it isn't going to make them want to hire you or your law firm.

Instead, write your copy to help them make sense of their situation and understand what's likely to happen if they go down the left fork in the road versus the right versus just standing there at the point of decision forever while the rest of the world leaves them behind—"This is what's probably going on in your life right now if you have this kind of problem. This is what's probably going to happen. These are your options. These are the likely consequences"—and help them make a decision as to which course of action is going to be more impactful for them. That's what selling in person and selling in print is all about.

We have each sold many, many tens of millions of dollars, both in person and from our copywriting, and we promise you, it really is this simple.

SELLING AN APPOINTMENT VERSUS A DIRECT-TO-SALE OFFER

Most of what we've discussed so far in the Conversion System is based on the idea of using all these components to lead up to a direct engagement of your firm. The power of building this out into a sequential step-by-step process, with the Lead Generation Magnet at the very beginning, leading to one after the other, is that it creates a foundation for the prospect saying "YES" through an ongoing series of microagreements.

- ➔ Prospect says YES to the Lead Generation Magnet.

- ➔ Then says YES to opening a follow-up email and watching an online video.
- ➔ Then says YES to taking an assessment sent in the mail.
- ➔ Then says YES to reading a book sent to his home.
- ➔ And so on ...

All these YES agreements build on one another, leading the prospect to feel more and more in agreement with what you have to say and offer. And of course, protecting you from those who don't. So when the final call to action appears, they already feel a sense of trust and rapport. Plus, they've established an almost hypnotic habit of saying YES to what you put before them. Of course, this doesn't guarantee the sale, but it absolutely makes it much more likely. People want to believe they behave with consistency. If you can get them to consistently say YES, you have started the ball rolling in the right direction.

Ultimately, in most cases, the actual sale requires "selling" the prospect on agreeing to attend some kind of in-person or telephonic, interactive, one-on-one consultative meeting.

> **All of these YES agreements build on one another, leading the prospect to feel more and more in agreement with what you have to say and offer.**

In these kinds of scenarios, you're using components of your Conversion System to lead directly to making that appointment—and this could involve the multistep campaign, Shock & Awe box, ongoing content, etc.

The appointment is where you—one-on-one—work with the prospect through their specific situation and craft the appropriate solution to meet their needs. The Call To Action at the end would be to sign the engagement agreement and make payment arrangements.

It's important to keep this clearly in mind. If the prospective new client does not engage your firm to help them solve their problem, then they haven't really set in motion a series of steps that are going to lead to a solution to their problem. Most lawyers who are struggling financially give up at this point and leave their prospective new client to his or her fate. Just think for a few minutes how ridiculously inefficient (and unprofessional) this is.

They've invested time, money, and energy figuring out how to get the prospective new client to a meeting either by telephone or in person. They've juggled their schedule around to prioritize their meeting with this prospective new client, likely making apologies to friends, family, and other clients to make the time for this meeting. They know the prospect has a problem that's not going to go away on its own and it's likely to deteriorate/not improve by delay or inattention. And so what do most lawyers do at the first "no"? They give up.

Setting aside the inefficiency and wasted time, money, and energy, let's just take a minute to consider how unprofessional, unethical, and downright unkind it is to leave a person to his or her fate when you know what likely lies ahead but they don't.

Imagine you're walking toward a steep cliff with a long drop off that ends in a pit of alligators at the bottom. We know what's about to happen to you because we've been in this business for decades, but this is all brand new to you. It's your first time being arrested, immigrating to a new country, dealing with a divorce, starting a new business, buying a home, taking a new idea to market, etc. We know you're about to walk off a cliff to your doom, but you don't. In what world is it professional, ethical, or humane to let you walk off that cliff without doing all we can to stop you and show you the ladder that you don't know about?

So instead of doing what most lawyers do who struggle financially year after year, YOU are going to follow up and follow up and follow up. And your Magnetic Conversion System is going to help you keep delivering MORE content, MORE Shock & Awe, and MORE multistep campaigns of email/direct mail/postcards/etc. More, more, more until you help the prospective new client find the courage to solve the problem!

How long should you keep this up?

As the old saying goes, "Until they buy or die," or they simply tell you to stop.

Now, once someone does become a client, we don't want our magnetic attraction to fade. For this reason, we continue with the Magnetic Lifetime Value Maximizing System.

CHAPTER 9

Your Magnetic Lifetime Value Maximizing System

This is the part of the puzzle that hardly anyone else is doing. But you can! And hopefully you will. Because this is the part that can quickly and easily maximize the lifetime value of each new client who engages your law firm, turning one engagement into a series of engagements and one client into two, thus increasing the value of every new client exponentially! Which of course means you can give yourself an enormous competitive marketing advantage. Just imagine what it means for your marketing budget when each new client is worth four times more to your firm than any other. And best of all, this is the easiest system to implement in your business.

One of the most important keys to maximizing the lifetime value of a client of your law firm is to think in terms of lifetime value, not transactional value like most law firms do. Most lawyers are out there trying to get a client so they can get work out of the client. The entire *Magnetic Marketing for Lawyers* System turns that on its head and has us looking for any opportunity to do something of value for a person—even if it's for free—in order to EARN THE RIGHT to call that person a client.

Yes, we know this isn't exactly consistent with how bar rules are written. But it's not violative of how bar rules are written either. In fact, we think our approach, which we've shared with thousands of some of the most ethical, professional, and profitable lawyers in the country, actually exceeds and surpasses the minimum floor set by bar rules! Isn't this exactly how you'd prefer to be thought of by YOUR lawyer? Even after the instant case or matter is concluded, the client's life or business continues, and it can continue to benefit from our care, consideration, and ongoing interest.

After all, who knows more about what to expect in the months or years that follow final discharge in a bankruptcy matter, the final judgment in a divorce decree, following the verdict in a trial, entrance to and release from custody in a criminal proceeding, granting of citizenship, granting of a patent, closing on a new business or a home (buyer's or seller's side), and on and on and on? Who knows more about what the client will face next and next and next again than YOU, a lawyer who sees this sort of thing day in and day out?

So, it is a matter of common decency or smart and strategic marketing to invest in building out a system that maintains top of mind awareness and keeps your law firm relevant in the life of the person or business whose trust your work has earned you the right to call a client.

After their case is closed, your client (no longer a "prospective new") is going to be eager to get on with his or her life. And remember what we discussed earlier about the fact that most people don't know a lawyer and they don't even know anyone who knows a lawyer? Well, your clients are all unique in that regard. Because they all know a lawyer, and not just any lawyer—they all know a lawyer who now takes an active interest in the ongoing affairs of their life and business.

Keeping your position "top of mind" requires your firm to remain relevant. Your firm can remain relevant by asking the right questions at the right time(s).

For example, Dan has made a fortune helping cosmetic surgeons devise highly effective marketing campaigns. And one of the things that cosmetic surgeons know is that a good time to present the option of cosmetic surgery to a prospective new patient is about eighteen months after their divorce is finalized. This isn't necessarily politically correct, but it's valid and backed up by testing and hundreds of millions of dollars' worth of sales as proof.

If you have been practicing in your area of the law for any number of years, you should be able to think about and make a list of a dozen milestones you've seen hundreds of clients come upon after the conclusion of their case or matter.

- ➔ Many (not all) women who get divorced are especially receptive to offers to improve their physical appearance about eighteen months postdivorce; many (not all) men are in the market for a new vehicle—and not just any vehicle; statistically it's likely to be a sports car or a pickup truck.
- ➔ Many (not all) bankruptcy clients within three to six months following discharge are going to be in the market for a new vehicle, new sources of credit, and improved housing options.
- ➔ Many (not all) clients who close on a new home within thirty to ninety days are going to be looking for a decorator, new furniture, and any number of different types of tradespeople—preferably someone who comes recommended by someone they can trust, like the lawyer who helped them close on the house.

We could fill a book with examples like this for every practice area. People tend to wind up hiring the services of every different type of lawyer because of certain predictable behaviors and choices that they make—and they tend to have certain problems and opportunities and face certain choices following (arguably even because of) the services of those very same lawyers. And their lawyers are in the extraordinarily unique position to be able to recognize these patterns, to be in a position of authority to guide and advise what comes next, and next and next again after that … for years to come. Except most don't.

We can remain relevant so long as we're either asking or, better yet, answering a very simple BUT POWERFUL question that is so important to us as human beings that it has become part of our vernacular. It's how we greet each other. That question is:

"What's new?"

You don't say, "Tell me everything that's the same as it was the last time I saw you three months ago."

No one is interested in that. We're all interested in *"What's new."*

If you don't have a good answer to "What's new?" they go looking for it somewhere else. A bored client goes elsewhere. They forget about you. They don't talk about you. They don't return to you for repeat business. And they don't make many referrals to your law firm. Instead, they are easily wooed by some competitor who comes along with something that's new and exciting … and that competitor doesn't even have to be a law firm!

How do you answer this question that is always on their minds? And how do you do it consistently and repetitively, so they are always intrigued by you?

The answer is to be proactive. That's it. Don't do like most lawyers do, waiting around for the phone to ring while flattering themselves: "If any of my clients from the past has a need for my services, they'll call me." NO, THEY WON'T!

Instead, they'll probably live with the problem for a lot longer than they should, until it gets worse. Or they'll open up about their new problem to someone else who may not even know you. And that person may refer them to another lawyer whom they do know—not you! Or your former client may not even know they have a problem or an opportunity at all. The point is, it's that unique convergence of arrogance, naivete, and entitlement demonstrated by lawyers with underperforming law firms everywhere to expect that whenever anyone whose case or matter you may have resolved years ago ever has anything new come up in their life or business that you'll be the first person they call.

A Magnetic Marketing System maximizes lifetime value by being proactive about keeping your firm top of mind. And we do this by creating a system that asks, educates, and/or tells your "former" clients what's new in their life or business or what to expect in their life or business that we know about based on our experience with so many other people who were similarly situated in the weeks, months, or years following their case or matter. There are also all the holidays you can help your clients anticipate and plan around too.

And you don't have to—should not—limit your thinking to their legal issues.

- ➔ **Help your divorce clients with tips or even a referral in preparation for their first round of holidays following that divorce you helped them get. Guess what all the other divorce lawyers are doing for their clients leading up to the holidays, if it doesn't require a law license to do?**
- ➔ **Send a housewarming gift to all the clients whose closing your firm handled, and then follow**

up with helpful tips and offers for a referral nine months later when you KNOW they'll be thinking about renewing their insurance. Better yet, don't wait that long ... follow up in ninety days after they've closed to see if you can help them find reliable tradespeople.

- ➔ Put all your clients on at least an electronic, better yet a paper, newsletter subscription with articles that are NOT about the law but rather about the life of a person who has just immigrated to this country, bought a business, sold a business, filed a patent, etc., etc.

OUR NEW WIDGET:

This may not necessarily be appropriate for every practice area, but in most it's not only perfectly appropriate but even appreciated when you keep your firm relevant by frequently and continually reinventing your business, inventing new widgets, talking about issues that are relevant to your clients' lives and businesses—not just legal issues—and offering those resources through constant communication with your past and present clients.

At least once a month, if not more often, they should be hearing from you about something relevant and getting a new widget offered to them. This will keep all clients interested and engaged, trigger more repeat business and more referrals too!

Point is, your complete *Magnetic Marketing System* should incorporate what in direct-marketing lingo is called "front end and back end."

1. *Front end* refers to outreach to attract and acquire new leads, new potential clients, and new clients.
2. *Back end* means developing and retaining those clients, increasing the frequency of repeat business you do with them, cross-selling different services—even the services of others in your network—putting fresh offers in front of them frequently, staying interesting to them so they stay with you and tell others about you.

Most of this book leading up to this chapter was about front end marketing. This chapter is all about back end marketing.

Eventually, your back end marketing system will evolve into a very sophisticated machine that will produce hundreds of thousands of dollars of repeat and referral revenue for your law firm every year and, if you're of a mind to do so, then millions of dollars of repeat and referral revenue to your law firm every quarter! But we have to start somewhere. And two of the quickest, easiest, and most cost-effective things you can do to instigate new business for your law firm consistently every year include Client Newsletters and GAS Calls.

1. Client Newsletters

Every firm should have some kind of client newsletter that—at a minimum—hits their doorstep once a month. Preferably it would be a real, printed newsletter. Electronic obviously requires less investment, but it's not going to be nearly as profitable as paper and ink in hand.

Why?

First off, paper and ink in hand has a higher perceived value—a physical newsletter just looks like it has more value than an email. Secondly, it's more likely to get consumed. An email—maybe it gets delivered, maybe not. Maybe it gets opened, maybe not. And if it does get opened, it better be short because it only has until the next distraction to get consumed before being closed with the best intentions of getting back to it or deleted straight away. But if you get something in the mail that you have to open up and look at and it's at least minimally fun and interesting, then it's far more likely to get read and possibly even retained.

Stories abound from lawyers (and each of your authors, too) of highly profitable clients returning after years lost with an old paper newsletter in hand and the same story over and over again: "I carried this thing around with me for months."

And that brings up the third reason a real-life, honest-to-gosh print newsletter has value—if they keep it around, it lingers as an ongoing reminder of your existence. You're no longer a memory of some service once rendered. You're there on the corner of the desk, in the briefcase, on the file cabinet keeping your former client company and letting them know you're still around.

Your monthly client newsletter should include:

- **Content that reaffirms your uniqueness (remember that USP?) and authority in your firm's area of expertise. But keep this minimal, as little as absolutely necessary. (For heaven's sake, do NOT make your entire newsletter about the law. Nobody wants to hear about "how trust fund management has changed thanks to the latest ruling of the blah, blah, blah" from their** estate planner.) Remember your audience! Remember the conversation that you know they are having in their heads—continue to talk about practical problems you know that they have.

- Content that's fun for the sake of being fun—puzzles, brainteasers, jokes, recipes, cartoons, funny "memes," lighthearted fodder that offers some entertainment value. You want your clients to look forward to this every month. Puzzles and brainteasers are also what we call engagement devices. Meaning that your newsletter will have staying power while they are engaged with it.
- In line with "What's new?" some kind of call to action for your latest widget. You are in business, after all, and you want to constantly remind clients that you offer solutions and services that will eliminate worry and fear and make their lives better. This is a great place to offer your newest consumer report or special report on a newsworthy topic that is plaguing them.
- And finally, personality. When you create a bond with your clients, they are less likely to choose a competing attorney over you because you have become a friend. Your newsletter allows you to continue your relationships. By telling stories and sharing what is happening in your life, you let your clients bond with you.

BONUS: Visit HowToManage.com/MagneticNewsletter to download a free template for a very ugly, very simple, and very effective (read "profitable") newsletter that any busy lawyer can produce in less time—with more business coming from it—than you may already be spending writing articles or attending networking events!

2. GAS Calling Your Firm's Clients for Life!

Remember when we mentioned the GAS (*give a shit*) concept of touching base with your clients? Here's a quick strategy to generate some fast new business using the Magnetic Marketing principles that also pays long-term dividends. It's all based on the idea that your clients have lives and business interests that extend far beyond just the legal matter you may have handled for them. So we pick up the phone—eventually you'll learn how to do this and prove to yourself that it works reliably enough to let someone else pick up the phone for you—and you call your former clients with an opening that goes a little something like this:

> "Hello; is this NAME? Hi; this is LAWYER. Don't worry—there's nothing wrong and you're not going to get a bill for this call. It's just that it's been about a year/about six months/about two years/about three months/it's getting toward the end of the year/it's the start of a new year, and we like to check in with our clients at around this point after their case has closed to go over some things that many of our clients tell us come up about a year/six months/etc. after their divorce is finalized/moved into their new home/get sworn in as a US citizen/get their patent filed. Do you have about twenty to thirty minutes

> to go over some things I'd like to check in with you about now, or can we schedule a call for another time?"

> **BONUS:** Visit TheGASCallCompany.com to download sample scripts and see and hear it all in action.

Now think about it. When's the last time anyone you entrusted with an important matter in your life or business, paid thousands of dollars to, and shared a whole bunch of private information with … when's the last time any of them ever called you to follow up about not just the thing they helped you with but some of the things that the thing they helped you with logically connect to? Probably never. This is why this is such an enormous opportunity to show up and keep showing up like nobody else! Once you get the hang of it, you'll find you can turn it into a low-cost/high ROI machine that keeps working for you day in and day out, even while you're away from your office with "Emergency Access Only."

When you find some correlations among the clients your GAS Calling System uncovers, why not create a free resource such as a two- to three-page PDF resource/report to solve that ONE problem and then a video to tell the world about it—here's the basic script:

> "I have been talking to my clients. And it seems that right now many people (describe your ideal client) are thinking about/worried about/excited about/have questions about (whatever the problem is). They're telling us they're feeling (describe what they're telling you). And that is why our firm has created (NAME OF FREE RESOURCE). So you can X, Y, Z (Benefits) and then CTA (call to action) to get this resource for FREE simply by XXXXX (tell

them what to do) and ask them to share this resource with people around them whom they know need help."

Then you can repurpose that video on your YouTube channel and whatever social media channels you're using to market your business and even write a short article about it for your newsletter.

RINSE AND REPEAT.

CHAPTER 10

Applying the Magnetic Marketing Systems

To borrow from Charles Dickens, we're going to wrap up here with the "Tale of Two Lawyers."

The story of these two lawyers is really important because it makes clear the sharp contrast between how most attorneys attempt to market their firm versus how an attorney who understands and embraces the concepts of Magnetic Marketing approaches that effort.

So, with that said, here is:

"A TALE OF TWO LAWYERS"

Consider this tale of two lawyers we know. These are based on two very real law firm owners we know. But for obvious reasons, we've anonymized the details to protect the guilty.

Both are in their early forties, both are happily married with great kids about the same ages. Both practice in similarly sized markets in the same area of law. And even though this story revolves around one particular area of law that they both practice in, we trust by now you know enough to recognize the area of law doesn't matter in the least as this same story plays itself out thousands of times all over the country in all different practice areas.

We'll call them Andy and Betty.

Andy and Betty both graduated from good law schools with good grades. They both got good jobs at good law firms, where they had good mentors who taught them how to be very good lawyers.

Around the same time, five years ago, for totally different reasons,

Andy and Betty each decided to start their own law firm.

Andy thought he could make more money on his own and have a bigger positive impact on the world practicing law "his way." So he rented space in a small office in his hometown and got down to business.

Betty had hit the glass ceiling one too many times and had been left out of too many important meetings that took place at the urinal; plus, she found herself unofficially on "the mommy track" after giving birth to her second child. Finally fed up, Betty left to start her firm in the same town as Andy at around the same time.

Andy's Story

Andy believes that all it will take to be successful is to first and foremost be a great lawyer, do the same kinds of marketing his peers do, that as a result plenty of clients and cases will show up on his doorstep.

He doesn't want to limit in any way the types of clients and types of cases he takes, which is made abundantly clear by the slogan on his business card, which might as well say, "Door Law for Anyone Who Can Pay Me." And because he figures the majority of his business will come from referrals, he has printed a little note on the back saying, "Referrals Welcome!" He thinks that's pretty clever.

Andy puts up a website (with the help of an agency who promises to put him on the first page of Google) loaded with every keyword phrase associated with "legal" possible—"divorce attorney," "estate-planning attorney," "wills and trusts," "accident victim," "workers' rights," "criminal defense," and so on. The site makes it clear Andy's little law firm is willing to handle everyone and everything—in fact, he went out of his way to be sure there was nothing on the website that could possibly dissuade anyone with any kind of legal problem from picking up the phone and calling for an appointment—and the sooner, the better! The site focuses on Andy the Lawyer, the schools he went to, and even has a professionally done photo of him at his office in front of a bookshelf crammed with legal books.

Andy runs an ad in the local newspaper that looks exactly like the same ads most of his peers use ... he doesn't want to stick out like some kind of weirdo. It lists his phone number and offers a "free consultation," just like everyone else does.

He does manage to get clients, and he does provide them with excellent service, but once their case is finished, there's never any kind of continued outreach. After all, Andy did a great job; he's sure they'll remember him when it comes time for any other legal services they may need. And besides, Andy doesn't want to be "pushy."

Andy does all the things he was told by all the other lawyers at his local bar association that they're doing to bring in business—being a great lawyer, putting ads in the paper, sponsoring a Little League team, going to local networking events, and so on.

But after five years, Andy's law firm is still just him and an assistant working out of three rooms. He hasn't taken a vacation in years. And lately Andy notices that he's begun making fewer long-term strategic decisions about where he wants his business and his life to be ... and more tactical decisions about how to make payroll and rent at the end of the month. Of course, Andy doesn't turn down any business, and so after five years he's handled about 100 divorces, 150 criminal matters, and a few dozen bankruptcies. Andy also writes wills once in a while and handles the occasional real estate closing. Andy is broke, worried all the time about where the next case will come from, and professionally unfulfilled. But he is very popular among his peers because Andy is a good guy and good lawyer.

Betty's Story

Betty studied the principles of *Magnetic Marketing for Lawyers.* She understands that she can't be all things legal to all people, so she decides to narrow her focus on helping the clients with whom she already has a natural affinity—professional women who have experienced workplace discrimination.

She thinks long and hard and creates a USP specifically for this demographic: *"I am the lawyer I wish I could have hired when I ran into the glass ceiling—I GUARANTEE you'll be treated with the care and respect you deserve."*

Betty creates a widget and headline that also speak to her WHO: "*If you're a woman and you've faced illegal job discrimination, call XXX-XXX-XXXX today to get my free report—'Know Your Rights: Seven Strategies to Make Sure Your Employer Treats You Fairly … And What You Can Do About It If None of These Seven Strategies Work for You!'*"

Betty does many of the same things as Andy—she buys an ad in the local paper, she attends networking events, she sponsors a Little League team, she builds a website.

The key difference is that she makes sure that EVERY place she shows up, she promotes her USP and her widget.

Betty's website has a pop-up offering the widget to any visitor who happens to find her. She also included targeted keywords for her website to help with SEO but didn't bother to include keywords for legal services that aren't top of mind for her ideal target client. She also builds up SEO by blogging regularly on the topic of workplace discrimination—and only on this topic—each post including the keyword phrases she knows her prospects use to search for help and each post including a call to action to grab her widget.

There's a long video of Betty on the site—all her friends from law school tell her it's too long and that she looks too "unprofessional" because Betty tells her own personal story and gets emotional when she does. Betty's video is eight minutes long, and indeed it's a major turnoff to everyone, but the only type of people Betty really cares about—professional women who have been discriminated against in the workplace—they can't get enough!

Betty not only provides great services to her clients, but she also makes sure to remain in touch with her printed client newsletter, which goes out every month via US mail. It's interesting, fun, and keeps Betty top of mind whenever they or someone they know needs a lawyer.

After five years Betty has handled more than 250 cases of professional women who have been discriminated against in the workplace. She has checklists and templates, and everyone on her team knows just what to do because these cases represent about 80 percent of what the firm does. Even the reception area is tailored to the unique needs and sensibilities of professional women who have been discriminated against in the workplace. It doesn't look very "professional," but when an unemployed woman with young children needs to see a lawyer, it's not always so easy to find childcare, and Betty's clients love that they're welcome to bring their kids, who love to play with all the toys and games that Betty's staff maintain in a spare room they call "The Kids' Office." Betty's reputation has spread, revenues have steadily grown—enabling her to add team members—and now she's looking for a third associate so the law firm can help even more women and handle even more cases.

One of the first résumés Betty sees is from another lawyer in town, named Andy …

What REALLY Happened Here …

Now that we've told the little tale, it's important you understand what's going on in the life of the main character around whom this story and every other story about the successes or struggles of a law firm revolve.

The CLIENT.

Remember, as you step into the story of their life, they are the center of their story, not you, not your impressive diplomas or fancy office. The client is the center of his or her own story, not you. You serve a critical role as their advisor, counselor, guide—there to help them navigate through the challenges and drama taking place. But it's not your story the client is interested in. It's their own.

And they need you and need you to market as effectively as possible because your prospective client has a problem that only YOU as an attorney can help them solve ... and very likely YOURS is the only law firm in your area that is based on your unique philosophies, values, and point of view about how the world should be. In other words, yours is likely the only law firm in your area that can do more than "just" address the client's legal issues. Because the client is more than the sum total of their legal issues. The client is a whole human being—even if he or she is a human being in charge of deciding which law firm to engage for his or her business. There is simply no other human being exactly quite like any one of your clients, and each of those individuals is looking for a law firm unlike any other to be a good "fit" for them, not just to

> **The client is the center of his or her own story, not you. You serve a critical role as their advisor, counselor, guide—there to help them navigate through the challenges and drama taking place.**

solve their legal problems. If you can shove your ego aside and embrace this fact, it will be magnetic to the right sorts of clients even though it may repel the rest, and that's OK.

Your client is losing sleep over whatever situation caused them to be receptive to your message in the first place. They're worried about how it's going to affect their life, their family, their career prospects, their future—and likely none of the thoughts they have are positive.

This problem hangs over their life like the proverbial Sword of Damocles, always there, always a concern, haunting every waking moment and keeping them awake at night.

All of this causes the potential new client to begin looking for a solution. Of course the only time they've got to look for a solution is the middle of the night, because the problem is eating up all of their free time during the day—plus, they've got kids, a job, a relationship, a life, responsibilities.

So, there they are, awake at 3:00 a.m., and they're scouring the internet looking for a solution. Or it's 12:17 p.m. and they're sitting at their desk in the office during their lunch break. Or it's the weekend and they're glued to their cell phone while the kids beg for attention.

Hooray—they found your advertisement. They found it online. They found it in the newspaper. They found it in an old-fashioned print telephone directory. Or maybe someone they know, like, and trust gave them your name and website address and they went to your website.

Except then their kid came into the room crying because a bumblebee bit them on the butt.

Except now one of their coworkers has come to their desk to ask a question about the bumblebee that bit their kid on the butt. Except now they are feeling extremely self-conscious looking at your ad because they're not in a place where they have a lot of privacy and their supervisor is nearby, potentially looking over their shoulder and wondering, "What's going on with her?"

What happens inevitably is the real world intervenes and throws a wrench into your marketing plans and you never even knew about it—because none of your marketing gave the prospective new client any cause to identify him or herself with your firm, and it certainly didn't give you permission to follow up in a bar rules–compliant way.

The next day the client loses more sleep over their problem and remembers that they saw your advertising "somewhere" the day before. They remember that their friend or other trusted advisor gave them your website and they wrote it down "somewhere." They take the initiative on their own to go back and find your ad (without getting distracted by anyone else's). They take the initiative on their own to go back to your website, where again they're given no reason and maybe even no way to let you know they're losing sleep and looking for a solution.

They've not learned anything helpful about their situation from you—no free report, no educational video, no invitation to an informative webinar, no nothing; they're just out there on their own, losing sleep, looking for a solution in their spare time.

THAT is the story taking place out there a million times over for real people with real lives struggling to solve real problems. And you—using typical advertising and marketing methods that you just sort of fell into because everyone else is doing it—are simply hoping that your prospective new client can make it through this gauntlet of distraction from friends, family, children, pets, coworkers, bumblebees, and customers of their own and everyone else in the world putting advertising in front of them, too.

Whoever ends up getting this client may end up flattering himself or herself it happened because of their sterling reputation, where they went to law school, how many cases they've won. (Do you really think any of your clients are going down to the courthouse to research this?)

Or they imagined the client chose them because of what a brilliant technician they are. (Do you really think your clients who didn't go to law school can recognize the difference between a brilliant technician versus a good enough technician versus a generalist who just got into this area of law yesterday because they're broke and thought the grass looked greener on your side of the bridge?)

And let's not forget all of those amazing lawyers who are sitting around waiting for referrals who imagine the client will find them and choose them in that way too.

Point being, whoever gets this client absent a trackable marketing system is going to make up every reason in the book why they got that client, most of which will be complimentary to themselves and completely wrong.

Of course, they'll also make up reasons why they don't get the client, which will also be completely wrong—but still complimentary to them (the client is just stupid, other lawyers aren't playing fair in their marketing, he has a better office, she has more money to spend on advertising, etc.).

We hope you'll keep "The Tale of Two Lawyers," Andy and Betty, always in mind to remember the sharp contrast between how most attorneys attempt to market their firm and how an attorney who understands and embraces the concepts of Magnetic Marketing approaches that effort, and how it affects all those prospective new clients out there in need of real help. You don't have to be like Andy in "The Tale of Two Lawyers" anymore, because you've discovered the answer: Magnetic Marketing.

NOW IT'S UP TO YOU

"When you come to a fork in the road, take it."

—Yogi Berra

There are three steps to positive change:

1. Awareness
2. Decision
3. Action

With this book, you have experienced Awareness. There is a better, more productive, more ethical approach to growing your firm by applied attraction rather than by pursuit; by focused, targeted marketing rather than mud-against-wall and hope, and by an organized system rather than random and erratic acts.

Now you face a Decision that is entirely yours to make. The legendary attorney Gerry Spence is well known for using this parable about the wise man and the smart-aleck boy in closing arguments. The wise elder made himself available every Saturday for the villagers to line up and ask for his advice. The boy resented his authority and developed a plan to humiliate "Mr. Know It All."

The boy captured a small bird and concealed it in his hands and stood before the wise man and asked if the bird in his hands was alive or dead. If the wise man said, "Alive," the boy intended to quickly crush it to death and let it fall to the ground. If the wise man said,

"Dead," the boy would open his hands and let it fly free.

But the wise man proved truly wise with his answer: "Son, that bird is in *your* hands." If you are reading these words now, then chances are you probably resonated with much of what you've discovered in this book, perhaps caught yourself nodding in agreement a few times; maybe there are even a few notes scrawled in the margins. You probably wish your marketing could be remade to be more "Magnetic." Whether or not you wake up a year from now still just wishing or congratulating yourself for having taken action to make your firm's marketing more Magnetic—and enjoying the rewards—is entirely in *your* hands.

Frankly, the person who reads but does not act is no better off than the illiterate dunce who cannot read—arguably worse! The person who endlessly procrastinates and excuses himself from decisive action is no better than the somnambulant sloth. Excuses or results—you can't have both.

The road to ruin is paved with good intentions. And as an old saying goes, "*If wishes were horses, every man afoot would ride.*" Creative, constructive action is what actually brings about positive change. So, act!

> **Creative, constructive action is what actually brings about positive change. So, act!**

There is good news about Action. Running a law firm today is challenging. It is easy to feel overwhelmed. Are you too busy just making a living to make any real money? Or create a better life? That is understandable but should be unacceptable. So, that is where the organization built around The Magnetic Marketing System for Lawyers® can step in, step up, and work right alongside you in implementing a series of dramatic breakthroughs. Those next steps are offered on the very next page.

You can soon own a profitable and predictable Magnetic Marketing System of your own … or … you can continue as you are.

That bird is in *your* hands.

VISIT US ONLINE TO ACCESS THESE VALUABLE RESOURCES

Register your book

To receive a free audiobook download PLUS our Magnetic Marketing Toolkit, which contains valuable downloads and worksheets to help you create your own Magnetic Marketing System in your law firm, visit

- ➔ **MagneticMarketingForLawyers.com/Register.**

Test Your Magnetic Marketing Status

Curious about where you are on the Magnetic Marketing spectrum? Most law firms are doing marketing, but few are magnetically attracting clients with a fail-proof system.

- ➔ Take the Magnetic Marketing Quiz to find out at **MagneticMarketingForLawyers.com/SelfTest.**

The Magnetic Marketing System and Toolkit

First released twenty-five years ago—the Magnetic Marketing System and Toolkit has been the best-selling training kit for entrepreneurial attorneys who are interested in magnetically attracting their very best clients.

- ➔ Invest in the system at **MagneticMarketingForLawyers.com/System**

BONUS:

SUCCESS STORIES OF THE MOST SUCCESSFUL LAWYERS WHO HAVE CREATED A FLOOD OF NEW CLIENTS THAT PAY, STAY, AND REFER

JENNIFER HARGRAVE, FOUNDER, HARGRAVE FAMILY LAW, DALLAS, TX

Hargrave Family Law helps good people end broken marriages. We have been in operation since October 2017 and provide a full range of family law services, focusing primarily on divorce and specifically on Collaborative Divorce.

Conflict is a normal, and even healthy, part of life. However, as a human race, we are inept at handling conflict. My mission in life is to change the way we think about conflict. And it starts in the family. If we can't figure out how to handle and work through conflict in the most basic of human relationships—the family—what hope do we have to be able to resolve even more complex conflicts as a society?

I live and breathe conflict between spouses, and it is my life's work to find a better way to help families in conflict. Marriages don't fail because of conflict—they fail because of unresolved conflict. Unresolved conflict not only destroys the lives it impacts, but it also has a lasting legacy for generations.

WHO IS YOUR PRIMARY CLIENT?

The clients my firm works with value the family. The decision to divorce was not an easy one. It's often arrived at only after some pretty heroic attempts to save the marriage. Unfortunately, some marriages cannot be saved—often there are personality disorders, abuse, addiction. When my team helps a family transition through the divorce process without the collateral damage of warfare (which is how most divorces are handled), our clients are able to close a chapter in their lives and begin a new chapter of life, love, and success—not only for them but also for their children.

My firm's marketing is designed to attract prospective new clients who:

1. **Value the institution of marriage; and**
2. **Are selective in the battles they choose to fight; and**
3. **Want to preserve and protect the dignity of their family, including the spouse they are divorcing.**

Generally, these are sophisticated people who are successful in life. They often have an advanced degree or have advanced in life through their own ingenuity. They are creative. We represent about an equal number of men and women. Our clients have carried the weight of the success of their family, often disproportionately to the other partner.

And nothing makes me happier than to see our clients thrive after divorce. We offer people the opportunity to have a divorce that is consistent with their values and allows them to honor a significant part of their life that has now come to an end.

DESCRIBE HOW YOU DISCOVERED MAGNETIC MARKETING

I thought marketing meant trying to impress somebody with how "smart" or "successful" I am—I thought it was about showing off the accolades and letting them see how good our firm is at making sausage. My prior sales conversations were basically a tour of the sausage factory. And my firm's marketing was focused on me.

I have discovered the principles of Magnetic Marketing through my involvement with How to Manage a Small Law Firm.

Magnetic Marketing has taught me to get into the mind of my client. To think about what they are struggling with right now—to speak to those pain points.

Magnetic Marketing is focused on my client and the resources my firm has available to help our clients through one of the most difficult journeys in their life.

DESCRIBE HOW YOU ATTRACT YOUR IDEAL CLIENT

We offer a video about Collaborative Divorce that invites people who are interested to download the Collaborative Divorce Guide, which is followed up with a series of emails inviting them to schedule a consultation with the firm.

WHAT'S YOUR ENGAGEMENT PROCESS?

FIRST, they receive a confirmation email with the details of their appointment and the information we ask them to provide ahead of time ... which is not the same information most family law firms are asking for ahead of time. What we've learned from How to Manage a Small Law Firm is to ask for very different information that's completely consistent with Magnetic Marketing, and it has literally acted like a magnet by accelerating the prospective new client toward a decision to engage the firm even before they come to their first meeting with us!

SECOND, they receive an email with a video from me—talking about what to look for when hiring a family lawyer. This helps set their expectations, gives them criteria by which to evaluate us, or any family law firm, and keeps accelerating them—like a magnet—toward wanting to hire our firm and only our firm.

THIRD, they receive a phone call the morning of that confirms their meeting (and follow-up for any info we haven't yet received).

Prospects will meet with an attorney for a "paid for" consultation. The fee is $350, and they pay in advance when the appointment is booked. Before we began using Magnetic Marketing, it was much more of a challenge to get appointments booked; now it's pretty much a nonissue for the right kinds of clients, which is pretty great too because it protects my team from having to meet with people who aren't going to resonate with what we do.

Following the consultation—if they don't hire right away—they go into one of three buckets:

OPTION A: Firm declined representation. Client was not a fit. We send a confirmation email that we are not going to accept their case. We likely will not pursue any future correspondence with this individual.

OPTION B: Client declined representation—client not interested in firm. We send a follow-up email thanking them for considering us. They will also be added to our newsletter emailing list. And we schedule them for a follow-up call to check with them in a few weeks to see how they're doing because we really do care.

OPTION C: Client interested but not ready. We have a series of emails to nurture this relationship and help provide additional resources to them. We will also follow up with phone calls and will add them to our newsletter emailing list. Before I discovered Magnetic Marketing and How to Manage a Small Law Firm, I would have thought this was too "pushy." Now I realize it's really the right thing to do to follow up with a person who is going through a very tough time.

DESCRIBE HOW YOU STAY IN TOUCH

We publish a monthly newsletter that is sent by email to everyone in our list (past clients, current clients, friends, family, referral sources).

KEY TAKEAWAYS

- ➔ I have to get into the mind of my client. I have to know—where do they shop for groceries, where do they shop for clothes, what are they watching at 2:00 a.m. when they can't sleep, what kind of car do they drive, where do their kids go to school, what are their hopes and dreams? The idea of building an avatar was brand new to me when I joined How to Manage a Small Law Firm; now I can't imagine how anyone could run a law firm without doing this exercise!
- ➔ Marketing is not something we do TO someone. It is something we do FOR people. I've learned that marketing is how I show my compassion for people who are suffering in terrible relationships. I've learned that it is MY RESPONSIBILITY to market, so that I can help more people. I've learned that not marketing is COWARDICE—I cannot hide out and keep my resources hidden because when I do, more people are suffering.

HOW HAS MAGNETIC MARKETING FOR LAWYERS CHANGED YOUR LIFE?

This kind of marketing has transformed the way we think about taking care of our clients—not just me, but also my whole team. We are building a relationship with our future clients in a way that feels safe to them. This is so important for a family law firm because if a client doesn't feel safe, they're not going to tell you the whole story, and that's always going to hurt your case. By building the relationship in advance, we get more candor from our clients, which helps us do a better job for them.

The Magnetic Marketing for Lawyers System has caused a total shift in how I think about the ways we can begin to build connections with people. "Anonymous intimacy" was a phrase I was recently introduced to—people who are struggling in painful marriages are often embarrassed and ashamed to admit they need help.

The Magnetic Marketing for Lawyers System helps us attract them into our fold, and now we have a way to begin taking care of them even before they hire us by sharing practical lessons and empowering messages of support and encouragement. This way, when they do become a client of our firm, it's a smooth and organic transition from prospective new client to fully engaged client to former client who is now in a much better position to refer other like-minded people to our law firm.

This is a titanic shift in the way I think about my business.

LIISA SPEAKER, FOUNDER, SPEAKER LAW FIRM, PLLC, LANSING, MI

Ours is an appellate practice. In one sense, we serve families who have had their lives upended by the trial courts. But in reality we also protect lawyers who have lost their case at the trial court level or who find their win being challenged on appeal.

I am committed to helping families maintain a stable custodial environment when children are involved because I believe that children's lives are better when their established custodial environment is stable and not disrupted based on the whims of a judge. In many of our cases, the trial court misapplies the law and changes custody without fully appreciating what that will do to the children and the whole family dynamic. So, in a sense, my larger mission … one of the reasons for my law firm to exist and why it must be a successful business, is to force trial courts to follow the law so that children and parents will be able to enjoy better-established custodial relationships.

I wanted to work at an appellate boutique law firm, but there weren't any in Michigan, so I started my own. When I started, I was doing Door Appeals (any appeal that came through my door). But over the years, my appellate practice has become more refined, and we now have our marketing dialed in to attract primarily family law appeals.

WHO IS YOUR PRIMARY CLIENT?

We have a unique marketing strategy in that we do not market to our clients directly. Our primary audience is family law trial attorneys who then refer their clients to us.

The type of client we want to attract is one who has obtained a ruling from the family law judge that they cannot live with (usually involving their children, but sometimes there are monetary issues at the center of it too). Our clients have often made some mistakes that turn the trial court against them, but they are essentially good people who love their children.

We market directly to attorneys rather than individuals because we are trying to protect ourselves from getting calls from people who do not have a viable issue to appeal. In the past, whenever we marketed to the public specifically for an appeal, we were inundated with calls from people who did not even have a case in the trial court, let alone an order (or anticipated order) that they might want to appeal. The family law trial lawyers who refer cases to us act as an important strategic filter that protects us from wasting valuable resources speaking with people who are never going to be and should not be clients of our firm. For this same reason, probably 95 percent of our outbound marketing goes to family law trial attorneys to ensure that those are the types of cases we are referred (rather than criminal appeals, for example).

DESCRIBE HOW YOU DISCOVERED MAGNETIC MARKETING

When I started, I really did not have a marketing plan.

My “marketing” was mainly networking so that I would be top

of mind among any and all of my colleagues who might need an appeal someday. It was a good long-term plan (say over five to ten years), but it didn't help bring in a flow of cases month after month.

My initial marketing also involved writing articles for legal publications, presenting at legal seminars, writing amicus briefs for organizations (pro bono) in the Michigan Supreme Court. All of these gave me huge credibility over the long run but did not pay the bills from month to month. It was also very labor-intensive and didn't leave much time to actually practice law, manage my business, or have a life.

I was investing a tremendous amount of time in my so-called marketing, but it was not producing clients. It was all very unfocused. This meant that I was not helping as many people (pre-2017 we were bringing in perhaps two cases per month). The low case numbers obviously affected me financially; I also found it professionally dissatisfying because I knew we could be (should be) helping a lot more people!

I was introduced to the Magnetic Marketing concept by RJon Robins at the very first How to Manage a Small Law Firm workshop I attended in September 2016 (Blood, Sweat, and Tears—he even gave us a homework assignment to come up with a landing page campaign). But I sat on it for two years.

We incorporated Magnetic Marketing for Lawyers into our practice in May 2018. That was when one of my Practice Management Advisors at How to Manage a Small Law Firm finally managed to push me to develop my first e-blast/landing page/white paper campaign. I was very resistant to all of this because it's so different from "the way things are usually done."

We started sending e-blasts with landing page links to family law attorneys on a regular basis. Our cases and revenues increased almost immediately and have continued to increase dramatically since then. In fact, we started that first campaign right as we were heading toward a cash crunch, and it pulled us out of that cash crunch—it was like a miracle! I think if it hadn't been for that looming cash crunch, I might not have been willing to give this a try.

The approach we use now is even better—we use a system of sending out a white paper every month to family law attorneys. We stay top of mind with a select group of attorneys whom we know we want to receive referrals from. Because we have a defined market, we are able to deliver a lot more value that's very targeted to help them in very practical ways through a series of white papers that address issues of great relevance to a family law attorney. Most of what we're putting out there probably isn't of much use to non–family law attorneys, but the family law attorneys absolutely love it. As an added benefit, it requires a lot less attorney time to write a white paper that's only for family law attorneys than try to write something generic that appeals to a wider audience. The lawyers we've selected to focus our attention on really appreciate all the help we're giving them.

DESCRIBE HOW YOU ATTRACT YOUR IDEAL CLIENT

In April of 2018, we started sending out white papers to our Michigan family law firm mailing list. We would send out white papers via e-blasts every month to our potential referral sources. We started to send out white papers more often, at least once a month, as we have found that the majority of our referrals come from attorneys on our mailing list. We offer the white papers to trial attorneys for free, and the subject of the white papers is centered around appeals, preparing for an appeal, or how to help their clients avoid an appeal.

WHAT'S YOUR ENGAGEMENT PROCESS?

Our pre-engagement glide path starts with a lead calling our office (usually referred to by their trial attorney), or the trial attorney contacts our office directly. We take down the initial intake questions and do a conflict check, and if there is no conflict, then we evaluate the appeal, determine what type of appeal it is and if it's viable. If it is, then the New Client Coordinator conducts the sales call, drafts a fee agreement, and sends it to the Potential New Client. The PNC either signs or doesn't. Most of our sales take place over the phone or by Zoom, not in our office.

A PNC typically talks to our New Client Coordinator; if the referring trial attorney contacts us directly and requests to speak with me, then we will schedule it as a professional courtesy. The initial consult is free. But we do offer a limited number of paid consultations if a trial attorney just wants our assistance or guidance.

For those who do not immediately sign the fee agreement or sign within a couple days, our New Client Coordinator follows up with them regularly by phone and email. If the PNC contacts us while they are still in the trial court phase and we cannot represent them yet, we also follow up, but maybe a month or so after they call.

DESCRIBE HOW YOU STAY IN TOUCH

We have two different newsletters. The first is a quarterly newsletter we send out electronically to a mailing list of attorneys (which includes all our family law attorneys plus a select group of other attorneys we know). We then pick a county and send a hard copy of the newsletter to family law attorneys in that county. One of the lessons I've learned from How to Manage a Small Law Firm is that nothing is a failure if a lesson from it is learned, because everything is a test and we are still testing the ROI on electronic versus hard copy and county by county.

We have another newsletter for former/current clients that obviously speaks to a different set of concerns to keep it relevant.

The goal of both newsletters is keeping up Top of Mind Awareness and to keep giving people new "reasons" to contact our firm. Because the vast majority of our clients come from referrals, we want to make sure our potential referral sources know the latest happenings of our law firm, and we want to keep giving them (the referral sources) new reasons to refer business to us.

KEY TAKEAWAYS

- ➔ Helped me learn how to write the copy that will grab the attention of the reader and pique their interest and give them a compelling reason to contact me or have their client contact my firm.
- ➔ Taught me about "Marketing to the Wrong People." It seems like such an obvious statement. Of course, your marketing isn't going to yield the results you want if the people you are targeting don't want or don't need what you are selling. It amazes me how many lawyers I talk to nowadays have never been exposed to any of this and are just putting their messages out there totally oblivious to the market-to-message match concept. In fairness, we were oblivious to this critical concept too before we discovered How to Manage a Small Law Firm. But after reading

about the market-message-media triangle in the Magnetic Marketing for Lawyers System and thinking it over, we realized we were making that mistake. We were still trying to gain leads from the general population. The problem is the general population knows nothing about appeals. Now that we know that trial attorneys are our primary audience, we invest our resources more wisely, cultivating those referral relationships, and our marketing ROI is getting better and better!

HOW HAS MAGNETIC MARKETING FOR LAWYERS CHANGED YOUR LIFE?

It would be easier to explain in what ways the Magnetic Marketing for Lawyers has NOT changed my life for the better. The answer would be "none." Every part of my life is better now that my firm has a reliable system for attracting new clients. Magnetic Marketing for Lawyers enabled me to do something recently that I would have never dreamed possible when I joined How to Manage a Small Law Firm back in 2016. In 2019 I took thirty days out of the office to spend time with my family and travel. This year I am doing it again in spite of the pandemic. It is so meaningful to my children and my husband that we get to spend time together that is not just rushing around on a weekend or just one week out of town. And unlike last year, when we were traveling almost the entire time, this year, a chunk of my thirty days will be at home.

Our 2017 revenues were $644,000, and even with the cash crunch threats in 2018, our revenues still increased that year to $814,000. And in 2019 our revenues were $1,052,000.

We have done more Magnetic Marketing this year (2020) than ever before. And even though the pandemic has meant that courts aren't issuing orders (which also meant potential clients did not need an appeal), we are still on track to hit at least what we did in 2019, which is pretty amazing if you think about it. I couldn't be happier with my Magnetic Marketing for Lawyers System—well, actually I could, which is why I'm always testing and improving it just like RJon and Dan taught me!

SAMUEL DONCASTER, FOUNDER, DONCASTER LAW, PLLC, PHOENIX, AZ

The Doncaster Law Firm is an antifraud firm in Phoenix, Arizona. The firm helps people get their money back when they've been cheated in business and real estate deals.

Before launching this firm, I spent about ten years employed in other law firms. I always gravitated toward the fraud cases because I enjoy helping people recover after intentional wrongdoing.

I also developed a knack for it, and I noticed the number-one fear expressed by clients in fraud cases was fear that they couldn't have justice because the other side would lie and that it would be like the fraud was happening all over again. They didn't think it was possible to overcome the lie, but I never worried about that. I knew I could cross-examine any lie. Fraud trials satisfy my inner need to vindicate the truth—I guess you can say my commitment to the truth gives our clients the courage to stand up for themselves too and overcome the scariest part of their case.

Standing up for the truth has been a part of me for my whole life. For example, as a first grader, when the teacher mentioned Santa Claus, I declared to the whole class that Santa didn't exist. "He's just a lie big people tell to trick you into obeying them." I was a six-year-old Spartacus. But once I knew Santa wasn't real, I couldn't stand the thought of people, especially folks in authority, lying.

That's stayed with me to this day, and every day my team and I go to the office and defeat lies.

WHO IS YOUR PRIMARY CLIENT?

We have two primary avatars:

- "Ed" is a property owner who's had a successful career and made his money the right way, the honest way. He's always been honest in his own business dealings and has "Midwestern Values." He views the property purchase as a significant financial investment, and it represents the fruit of his labor. Ed learned that the seller made false disclosures in advance of the purchase and is worried about 1) how the lie he's now discovered will affect his property value, 2) the cost of repairs, and 3) how the fraud will affect his ability to build lifelong wealth and fund his retirement.
- "Carl"/"Carla" is a longtime entrepreneur who became a business owner at an early age. He or she has significant technical expertise and built a business around that expertise. Carla loves what she does. And the fact that someone has been dishonest roils her. She has significant business reasons for pursuing the fraud claim. But underneath the surface, she's more motivated by the fact that she just won't feel good about herself if she lets the bad guy get away with it.

DESCRIBE HOW YOU DISCOVERED MAGNETIC MARKETING

When I first started the business, marketing was my biggest challenge and I was terrified of it.

The lack of confidence that I could go get leads when I needed them held back every other part of my business. I didn't hire when I first should have, which ultimately started me on a revenue roller coaster. I delayed obtaining appropriate office space. I basically ran my business on the cheap until I couldn't anymore. Those fears associated with marketing were a big part of what held me back from growing the firm.

The worst part was the fear, though. Not knowing how I would find my next client scared me. When I launched the firm, the first "new" client I signed up (one who didn't follow me from the firm that employed me) was from an earlier referral. They had a decent case, and I won it for them in a few months.

But I knew something was wrong because I didn't enjoy winning that case the way I usually do. I realized that by getting aggressive and winning fast, I had just lost a client—because the case was now over. Talk about a conflict of interest! Because I didn't have anything in my pipeline to replace that client.

The other significant problem is that the fear of marketing held me back from growing my firm. The fear became a barrier to building a real business, and so for a long time I was really just in a job I made for myself. That job required me to spend more time than I liked doing the work of a janitor, a secretary, a receptionist. I needed something different.

I downloaded the How to Manage a Small Law Firm App and bought their business plan boot camp. It came with full access to the company's entire library of prior content, which I devoured—now I realize RJon had created what's called in Magnetic Marketing terms "a widget." Anyway, I'm a powerlifter and I do three to four long weightlifting sessions per week. So, I was listening to everything I could find on marketing while I lifted. On top of that, I listened to HTM content on the app whenever I was in my car, which was superconvenient, and two things happened:

1. I learned technical business skills, which included Magnetic Marketing, and that helped me grow my business; and
2. My mindset changed. I began to develop a vision and the confidence to put systems into place that will grow my firm to eight figures, not just seven, and I'm driving hard for that.

DESCRIBE HOW YOU ATTRACT YOUR IDEAL CLIENT

My lead magnet is a webinar—I'm usually testing different titles and topics—and once folks sign up, they get a series of autogenerated emails with all the details.

WHAT'S YOUR ENGAGEMENT PROCESS?

Once a client books an appointment, I do a pre-engagement glide path. It consists of two emails (one the day they book, the other the day before the appointment) that are full of practical material about how to find the office and attend the appointment.

I also send them three pieces of paper mail. Initially, these were done by FedEx. I'm changing it to lumpy mail for two of them, and

I'm including a notepad (to write down questions) and a pen (to write down answers to my client survey).

They get touched five times between booking and showing up, which really makes a big difference in not only the conversion rate but also how much less stressful the whole experience is for the client and for me and my team because when they show up, they already know what's what and they're thinking much more clearly compared to the way potential new clients used to show up before we implemented this system.

DESCRIBE HOW YOU STAY IN TOUCH

They typically meet with an attorney for a paid strategy session. Then, starting with the day of the consult as Day 0, the follow-up campaign (classic Magnetic Marketing for Lawyers sequence) goes like this:

- ➔ D+1—Follow-up call
- ➔ D+1—Mail paper letter (so they get it a few days later)—include case study
- ➔ D+4—Follow-up call; confirm receipt of letter
- ➔ D+7—GAS (give a shit) call
- ➔ D+10—Sales Letter—second case study
- ➔ D+14—Call

KEY TAKEAWAYS

- ➔ The importance of follow-up after an initial sales call. When I first started listening to his stuff, I didn't do that, and I was hovering right around a $200,000/year run rate. Less than eighteen months later, the firm is well over $25,000/month and we're even beginning to see $25,000 days! One of the biggest changes in my business has been post–sales call follow-ups. For a long time, I didn't even have a real system for it; I just did it. The simple act of staying engaged and continuing to show folks I care about them makes a big difference—plus, it's just the right thing to do.

- ➔ I learned that I don't need to self-filter or try to force myself to be politically correct to get clients. In fact, the more honest my marketing is, the more of our ideal clients step forward, and we don't worry anymore about the ones who step away because our Magnetic Marketing for Lawyers System keeps working for us day and night.

HOW HAS MAGNETIC MARKETING FOR LAWYERS CHANGED YOUR LIFE?

In under six months, the firm has had more than a 50 percent revenue boost, without any paid ads.

On a personal level, my dad recently visited and reminded me that a year ago, I was afraid to spend a dollar on anything because I didn't know where my next client was coming from. Now I'm looking to hire two additional associates because we have more work than I can do.

MARGARET BARRETT, OWNER/ FOUNDER, SAFE HARBOR ESTATE LAW, SAINT PAUL, MN

I started Safe Harbor Estate Law in 2013, back when I needed to support myself and my daughter due to a pending divorce. I chose Estate and Elder Law because my own life experiences gave me compassion, wisdom, and motivation to help people with aging parents or blended families or those who just wanted to provide for their families in the event of illness or death.

We help families protect what matters most by providing estate planning, estate and trust administration, Medicaid planning and application, asset protection for Medicaid, guardianship conservatorship, and special needs planning.

WHO IS YOUR PRIMARY CLIENT?

We're looking for smart, capable clients who are retired or approaching retirement, who know the value of paying for quality, who have built a solid legacy and want to make sure they don't leave a mess for their family after they are gone. They have approximately $1 million in assets. Old enough to realize how fragile life is, so they need to stop procrastinating. Generally fifty-five or older. I'm basically our avatar. Not only do I see daily the damage these problems cause to our clients' lives, but I have also experienced these problems myself personally and am very motivated to educate and empower others to avoid the problems or minimize their effects.

My children's dad (my ex-husband) died in a car accident at the age of thirty-nine. His estate plan was not up to date, and it wasn't prepared by an attorney who specialized in Estate Planning. As a result, we endured seven years of litigation that went up to the Minnesota Supreme Court. If he had had a Smooth Sailing Estate Plan like we customize for our clients, at least $100,000 of legal fees and so much heartache and hassle could have been avoided.

My current husband and I married almost three years ago, and as a member of a blended family, I knew the importance of having a good Prenuptial Agreement and updated Estate Plan to maximize the chance that our blended family will still get together after we are gone and that our money goes to both sides of the family.

My father died of dementia in 2019. My siblings and I worked together to care for him, and we still support my mom. I know the challenges and concerns of supporting aging parents, planning how to pay for their long-term care, and still respecting their independence.

I want clients in all of these situations to be able to rest their head on their pillow at night knowing they have done all they can to protect themselves and their loved ones.

DESCRIBE HOW YOU DISCOVERED MAGNETIC MARKETING

Long story short, I first discovered the Magnetic Marketing for Lawyers system when I engaged How to Manage a Small Law Firm to help me transform my practice into a real business. At the time, I didn't really know much of anything about marketing. I am basically the avatar—I was concerned about my aging parents and wanted to learn this area of the law for their sake, then I realized it was a great fit for me. Plus, I knew a lot of people who needed these services.

I took a speaking class and learned a little sales and marketing, and I networked ... a lot. But I had few clients. I had one free resource

I gave out to speaking attendees—at least I knew that much. But there was no pre-engagement glide path at all. No system for automatically following up with prospective new clients. My "systematic" approach was to return phone calls. And I did not follow up with people after the initial call or meeting. I don't even want to think about how much money I left on the table or how many more people I could have helped if I'd only learned about Magnetic Marketing for Lawyers sooner.

But at the time, it was just me and a contract paralegal, and I was working part-time. I wanted to delegate, to get away from the copy machine, to do what I was good at and have staff to do the rest, to have more freedom, and to build a law firm that would last—to fill the need I saw for Estate and Elder law firms in my town, ones that could relate to people as people.

Struggling to understand how to get more clients cost me lots of lost revenue, but I would say the personal and emotional impact of the stress and uncertainty about where revenue would come from was worse. Also, not having enough money to have a proper staff was tough. Four years ago I was in Europe for two weeks. My phone got stolen; I could not access my email or Google Voice for a couple of days. And I was the only person in my firm! That was stressful. Fortunately—or unfortunately, depending on how you want to look at things—I didn't have many clients or calls then, so nothing major happened, except that I felt I was failing my clients and losing business.

That is why I engaged How to Manage a Small Law Firm in October 2016, to help me upgrade my practice into a real business. My revenue that year was just $70,000. I did not know how to market to potential clients, and I needed to bring in more money so I could hire staff. I needed to bring in more money just to pay HTM's monthly retainer!

Now, thanks to the help my firm received from How to Manage a Small Law Firm on marketing and management, in just the first three years (2016–2019) revenues grew 900 percent and we landed #16 on The Law Firm 500 List of fastest-growing law firms in the country. Better than that, I now have a great team who can and do attend to each of The 7 Main Parts of a Successful Law Firm when I'm away from the office with emergency access only. But best of all, we are now able to help so many more people avoid the sort of problems I created this firm for in the first place; it's really a great feeling.

DESCRIBE HOW YOU ATTRACT YOUR IDEAL CLIENT

For lead generation, we use my signature talk (now a webinar) entitled "How Your Will (or no estate plan) May Be Failing You." We offer a free asset summary and Navigation Plan provided to attendees who want it and also offer a Life and Legacy Session. After the talk they get the asset summary and Navigation plan via email. Then we follow up with a call: "Did you get it? Do you have questions?" On that call we offer the Life and Legacy Session if they did not sign up for it. Then there's an email drip campaign for those who don't engage.

I also offer a two-minute video that is going gangbusters on Facebook right now: "The Main Difference Between Wills and Trusts." There's a free report that's a comparison of pros and cons of wills versus trusts. After the video they give their email to receive the pros and cons of will versus trust report. They are retargeted with other FB ads. By email, they receive drip campaigns including an invitation to speaking events (I just recorded a webinar with no live guests that we will add to this glide path so that they can sign up to watch the webinar any time, in addition to the live scheduled events). They receive the one- to two-minute videos, again with an offer of calling our firm or getting another report.

Everything is pointing to inviting them to a Life and Legacy Session. After we have their email, we ask for their phone number so we can call.

I love when people come to the firm and say my video really spoke to them, or my story on the website, or whatever it is—they remember whatever it is they heard that caused them to raise their hand for our firm.

WHAT'S YOUR ENGAGEMENT PROCESS?

Our goal is the Life and Legacy appointment; we are just adding other steps to help get them there if they are not ready yet. All ads have a different dedicated number to call, even if they offer a free resource, so we can track everything.

Next step is the prospective new client will normally have a conversation with our nonattorney salesperson (How to Manage a Small Law Firm calls them "Dragons") to make sure it is a good fit, and then our Dragon initiates an email sequence to further build the relationship. The basic path goes like this:

1. **They get an email confirmation of the appointment with a short explanation.**
2. **They get an emailed video of me explaining the first meeting, introducing myself (because they don't meet me at that first appointment).**
3. **They get helpful information about the appointment (e.g., how to pick the people**

you want to appoint as guardians, etc. so they're already thinking about this important question BEFORE they arrive for their meeting with one of our Dragons).

4. They get a very short intake form with about five questions, which is totally different than what most estate-planning law firms send to prospective new clients, thanks to what I learned from How to Manage a Small Law Firm and the Magnetic Marketing for Lawyers System ... ours works so much better!
5. They get an email with practical instructions (Zoom details or directions to the firm).
6. They get a reminder on the day of the appointment.

DESCRIBE HOW YOU STAY IN TOUCH

We have a "Did Not Engage" glide path. Assuming they are a client we want, they receive emails and scripted phone calls on a pre-scheduled basis. These include helpful information (could be recommended financial advisors or CPAs or other issues that came up during the meeting).

Plus, there are links to short videos, the webinar mentioned above, and our regular newsletter.

If the potential client indicates they will hire us, they are called daily until they sign and pay (unless they tell us otherwise). When this was first suggested to me, I thought it might be a bit much, but the proof is in the results, and the results prove that it works.

KEY TAKEAWAYS

- ➔ I have learned to have an avatar and to focus on their pain point. To care enough to ask questions, figure out what they are looking for. To create valuable tools to give away, to build trust, to sincerely want to help.
- ➔ I've also learned to develop a pre-engagement glide path, to track the numbers, to learn from them, to follow up and keep following up until they ask you to stop. And much more.

HOW HAS MAGNETIC MARKETING FOR LAWYERS CHANGED YOUR LIFE?

The difference has been day and night. From doing almost everything myself and having my husband cleaning the office to employing six FTE employees, having more income, freedom, ability to delegate and having great systems and benefits that I could not have come up with on my own.

Last year my revenue was $700,000, and in October 2019 I received the Law Firm 500 Award for sixteenth-fastest-growing law firm in the country. I have 6 FTE employees now, and we are continuing to grow. (NOTE: Along with most of the 400+ law firms that How to Manage a Small Law Firm was managing that year, Margaret's law firm continued to thrive during the pandemic of 2020.)

This was possible because I learned about and implemented Magnetic Marketing for Lawyers—identifying the potential client's feelings, providing them with some value at no cost to them, which is a great way to begin any relationship, then following up with phone calls, drip emails, newsletters, etc.

This summer I was able to pay $20,000 to landscape and put in a new patio around our pool; it is like a resort now, and I love entertaining family and friends. My firm has a good reputation. I do not stress about payroll and cash flow, and I work about forty hours a week, with vacations.

And here's the best part: my son just finished his first year of law school. He is learning the Magnetic Marketing for Lawyers System, running the Facebook ads, and I can leave him a firm that is solid and strong rather than struggling. That gives ME real peace of mind because that is part of my legacy to provide for him and his family now and in the future. Not only is he working for me four days a week and getting credit for learning to run a law firm, but my sixteen-year-old daughter is also working part-time for the firm and learning all about running a business too.

And my husband doesn't have to clean the office anymore, and do the banking, because I can afford to hire those services out.

I love being able to mentor my staff and help clients. But making a big difference in the lives of my family members is the best! Plus, now that I have systems I can rely on, I have more time to spend with them. I am fully funding my retirement account this year (the past couple of years I was investing heavily in growing the firm, buying and remodeling the office, etc.). Now it is time for profits. I am able to delegate legal work I don't like. My retirement looks rosy, and my son is going to have a great firm!

TOM SPIGGLE, FOUNDER, SPIGGLE LAW FIRM, ARLINGTON, VA

The Spiggle Law Firm helps people who have been wrongfully fired or are afraid that they might be. We have a focus on those experiencing pregnancy discrimination as reflected by our book, *You're Pregnant? You're Fired!*

I started the firm in 2009 because I was enamored with the "idea of doing my own thing." I eventually chose employment law because it was complicated and those coming into my office desperately needed help to save their careers.

WHO IS YOUR PRIMARY CLIENT?

Outside of family, the workplace is where we spend the most time and the place that forms much of our identity. Getting wrongfully fired can be a significant setback emotionally and financially. And the playing field is heavily tilted in favor of employers, who often have access to experienced counsel to navigate the situation.

The employee also needs expert advice to deal with the situation. Note that this does not often, or even most times, mean filing a lawsuit against the employer. It happens just as often that we are able to help the client to accurately identify their legal rights and steps they can take to negotiate a severance package and move on to something bigger and better.

We are trying to attract a client willing to take the time to educate themselves about the process and also those with significant economic damages. To make sure we focus on helping those who we can serve best, our *case assessment calculator* requires a number of steps and thus eliminates those not willing to take the time to educate themselves about the process. The follow-up emails are also designed to discourage those who think they have a winning lottery ticket just because they got fired.

DESCRIBE HOW YOU DISCOVERED MAGNETIC MARKETING

I first became aware of the concept in 2009 when I worked with RJon and his program *How to Start a Law Firm in 90 Days*. But it didn't take at the time. (So, so many mistakes!)

This cost me time away from my family. Negative health effects of high levels of stress. It also stalled out my career, as taking time babysitting high-need/low-value clients sapped me of the energy I needed to think about and work on the kind of practice that I truly wanted.

I revisited the concept of Magnetic Marketing sometime in 2013, when I started to read various marketing materials and follow marketing blogs and podcasts.

I started using this approach to marketing heavily and more effectively four to five years after opening my firm. Until that point I was often taking "C"—or even less favorable—clients that came to me from other firms. Taking less-than-ideal clients in a variety of different practice areas—I did not niche my practice to employment law until 2013—had predictable results. I was spending a lot of time on the phone with unreasonable clients, sometimes in areas of law that I was figuring out as I went along.

In 2013 I started with my first e-book, progressed to my current book in 2015, which I still use as a lead magnet, and then developed the case calculator in 2017. I paired these efforts with a content-heavy website and blog.

This targeted approach has continued to yield results, not only attracting more "A" clients but also generating more referrals from other attorneys who now better know how to refer to us.

DESCRIBE HOW YOU ATTRACT YOUR IDEAL CLIENT

Our ideal client is a midlevel professional woman with children who has excelled in her career but now is experiencing some real form of discrimination. She seeks fair treatment and wants to protect the career she has invested so many resources in. She may need a demand letter written, or she may just need help negotiating a severance package. If push comes to shove, she'll consider litigation. She makes over $70,000 per year.

Our most notable lead magnet is our free *case calculator*, which allows potential clients to get a rough approximation of what their employment law case could settle for based on average statistics in the field. After filling this out, they are directed to our short, accessible intake form on our website.

The leads are placed into a slow drip follow-up (one email per week) asking if they need any other services or information from the firm. They are tagged internally for future follow-up and lead magnets.

They also receive emails explaining the theory underlying the calculator and how an experienced attorney conducts a damages workup for an employment case.

WHAT'S YOUR ENGAGEMENT PROCESS?

Once the lead submits initial information on the website, they are reviewed and sent an immediate link to talk with a live representative about moving forward. Even if we choose upon review to not move forward with the case, the lead is sent an email packed with videos, free resources, and other useful information.

The lead is sent an initial questionnaire designed to allow us to get straight to business in their meeting. They are also sent event reminders via email as their meeting approaches.

Our prospects meet with a nonattorney salesperson during a no-cost consultation. No-shows are charged a $50 fee that is donated to charity.

DESCRIBE HOW YOU STAY IN TOUCH

Each nonattorney salesperson follows up with their appointments weekly via phone and email to make sure that all questions are answered and to see if the terms of the agreement can be further negotiated.

Our firm has a regular email newsletter that is sent on the first Friday of every month.

KEY TAKEAWAYS

- ➔ Taught me the concept of listening to your ideal client and trying to produce content that speaks to what keeps her up at night.
- ➔ Taught me the importance of good copy and writing headlines that speak to prospects' desires and pain points.

HOW HAS MAGNETIC MARKETING FOR LAWYERS CHANGED YOUR LIFE?

Using inbound Magnetic Marketing has been the primary driver of getting our firm over the seven-figure line, which has allowed us to develop a "real" business, one that does not require constant attention from the owner. This has allowed my wife to leave the big-firm job that she hated and for both of us to spend more time with our four children.

SARA KHAKI, FOUNDER, ATLANTA DIVORCE LAW GROUP AND THE KHAKI LAW FIRM, ATLANTA, GA

I am the Founder and President of two separate law firms. The first is the Khaki Law Firm, which I started in 2013 to help guide people through the maze that has become the Social Security Disability system. Today, the Khaki Law Firm is a seven-figure business that takes amazingly great care of its clients and runs day-to-day with Emergency Access Only to me.

I am also Founder and President of The Atlanta Divorce Law Group, which helps its clients find their Happily Ever After Divorce.® I started the second law firm in 2016 as a standalone brand because I had a specific opinion about how families could restructure during divorce and enjoy a healthier and happier future, rather than staying in a dysfunctional place. ADLG is also a seven-figure law firm with a completely different brand; it's managed with a separate P&L, and it has a completely different legal staff. The two firms do share one centralized back-office administrative team, which wouldn't be possible without the sort of systematic approach to law firm management that I learned from How to Manage a Small Law Firm ... that's one of the biggest things that appeals to me about Magnetic Marketing for Lawyers—it's a system.

WHO IS YOUR PRIMARY CLIENT?

Obviously, each of the firms has a completely different primary client. For ADLG—our primary client is a professional man or woman who demonstrates self-awareness and takes personal responsibility for their part in their unhappy family life. That's not to say they take the blame. Only that they're the type of person who takes 100 percent personal responsibility for their own happiness and success in life. This client understands that he or she stands to lose much more by choosing to fall victim to their unhappiness, to the patterns of their spouse, or to the legal divorce process. So, the messages we put out there about choosing instead to be at-choice throughout the divorce process and pursuing a better future for yourself and your family … they really resonate with the kinds of clients we want, and they really repel, even offend, some of the kinds of clients we don't want to work with.

Our ideal clients don't just wake up one day and decide to get divorced. A big part of their emotional journey involves information gathering to clear their conscience from any guilt or shame that they are quitting on their family. Part of their decision-making process is feeling they've done everything they reasonably could to avoid divorce and that divorce is now the only option left if they are going to have a healthier future for their family and themselves.

Many times we find our future clients at the stage where they are only seeking information on divorce but are not ready to "pull the trigger" because they still have not cleared their conscience and they're still looking for resources to save the marriage. Over and over again, they come in and tell us how much they appreciated the fact that we were willing to share resources and tools to help them to do their research on the divorce process and even on how to save a marriage if it can be saved.

DESCRIBE HOW YOU DISCOVERED MAGNETIC MARKETING FOR LAWYERS

I first became aware of the concept in 2013, when I engaged How to Manage a Small Law Firm to help me grow my first law firm, the Khaki Law Firm. For several different personal reasons, I wanted to upgrade that firm from a practice that I still had to work for every day and transform it into a real business that could work for me even when I was away for weeks or months at a time. The systems that the team at How to Manage a Small Law Firm helped me think through and put in place, which still run my business today, were a critical part of my now being able to do just that; and a big part of those systems—the marketing systems—they helped me put into place was Magnetic Marketing for Lawyers.

DESCRIBE HOW YOU ATTRACT YOUR IDEAL CLIENT

The Magnetic Marketing for Lawyers System helps us attract our ideal client in two important ways. The first is about timing. We focus on meeting our potential client at the emotional stage when they are still in the information-gathering phase of their journey. Most family law firms—most law firms, for that matter—don't show much interest in their potential new clients until the client is already past the information-gathering part of their journey. The second is about value. We make sure that any potential new client who comes into contact with any of our marketing material—whether they end up engaging our firm or not—gains something of value, even if the value they gain is knowledge or tools to save their marriage—yes, we are a divorce law firm that's doing a lot to prevent people from ever needing our services, and I think that's a pretty good thing!

We have multiple Magnetic Marketing channels we use that meet the two above standards. Three of them are our ***Get Ready Divorce Kit***, our ***Save Your Marriage If It Can Be Saved Kit***, and our ***Get Ready for Child Custody Modification Kit***. All three of these are downloadable PDFs geared to the potential new client who is not ready yet to hire an attorney but would like to prepare, know what to expect, and have their homework ready for when the time comes. Since our ideal client is a "doer" who likes to take action and not the type to just sit by and watch life happen to them, these kits really help them feel a sense of control and preparedness for what is to come. For the potential new client who wants to educate himself or herself about what to expect if they do file for divorce—or if they suspect their spouse may file for divorce—we offer our e-book: ***The Atlanta Divorce Survival Guide***.

In addition to the above, we also hold a quarterly webinar on various topics related to divorce, life after divorce, and child custody. We also sponsor a monthly support group that is run by a licensed family therapist.

WHAT'S YOUR ENGAGEMENT PROCESS?

Straight-up Intake System from How to Manage a Small Law Firm—once a potential new client calls us or fills out an online form from our website for us to contact them for a consultation, they will speak to our intake specialist on the phone for an initial screening to make sure they have a legal matter that we can assist them with and that they are in the correct jurisdiction for us to help. If the initial screening is passed, the intake specialist will schedule them for a consultation with a member of our team. An email is sent to confirm the appointment; the email also contains an electronic New Client

Questionnaire for the potential new client to complete and submit electronically. This questionnaire doesn't act like a sales prevention department by bogging them down with a bunch of technical questions best left for the actual consultation. Instead, it primes their thinking by asking important questions about their goals and priorities to help them begin to envision a better future. That way we start getting our prospective new clients in the right mindset before their consultation. Also, in this email, we attach directions to the office. Depending on for how many days out the consultation has been scheduled, there are a series of other emails that contain informational videos about our team, our mission at the firm, and what to expect from your consultation with us.

The day before the consultation a reminder phone call is made, and the day of the consultation, a reminder text message is sent out.

When the new prospective client enters our office for their meeting, a framed blackboard in our lobby will have a greeting welcoming the prospect to our office, with their first name on there. Our administrative assistant will welcome them by first name and offer them something to drink from our drink menu. While they are waiting in the lobby, a TV in the lobby will play a video where our client case studies and testimonials are being played, information about various members of our staff is highlighted, and a video that discusses our vision of Happily Ever After Divorce® is seen.

When it is time for the consult to begin, they are escorted to the conference room, where there are fresh, warm, baked cookies waiting for them and a folder on the conference table in front of the seat that we like for our prospects to sit in during their consultations. The folder contains a welcome packet that explains our external policies and procedures in working with our clients and also a branded notepad and pen for notetaking.

At the end of the consult, the person who conducted the consultation will hand to the prospect a branded gift bag that contains an ADLG-branded mug with chocolate inside, a personally addressed letter that comes from me, the owner, and the book *The Power of TED*. This book is about how to step out of dysfunctional cycles of drama and instead step into empowered relationships.

DESCRIBE HOW YOU STAY IN TOUCH

After the consult our intake specialist will receive a form from the team member who conducted the consultation that contains next steps. On that form the intake specialist will be asked to follow up in so many days, depending on what was agreed upon at the consult. Our intake specialist will use that as their benchmark for starting the follow-up process with the prospect, and this process will continue for months. In addition to follow-up phone calls, the prospect will receive our monthly newsletter and also an email drip campaign that continues to remind them of their options and the value of moving forward.

KEY TAKEAWAYS

- Has taught me to really think through and be clear on whom it is I want to work with as an ideal client and whom it is I want my firm to honor and to not be afraid to speak directly to that ideal client in our marketing material and be OK with polarizing the people we don't want to work with in the process. This allows us to create much more pertinent and profitable marketing material that will speak directly to the ideal client we wish to attract.

- Has taught me the value of slowing down the sales process by creating marketing material that does not constantly ask the prospect to "call now" or "hire now." Dan taught me to give more valuable tools and content to the client and give them ample material to continue to engage with the firm and to educate themselves, so that when they are ready to hire an attorney, they already trust you and see you as their trusted counsel whom they want to work with. This way, the sale is much easier and predictable because the prospect has already been sold on your firm through their longer engagement with your marketing materials.

HOW HAS MAGNETIC MARKETING FOR LAWYERS CHANGED YOUR LIFE?

Magnetic Marketing for Lawyers has allowed me to create two seven-figure law firms that attract the ideal client that my team and I love to work with. It has given us a framework to create marketing material that is personal and meaningful to us since it is designed to make an impact in our potential clients' lives in alignment with our firms' mission(s) and my vision as an owner.

Also, it has helped me create effective marketing systems that run without me and are so sharply directed at the right client, at the right time that we no longer have to throw away money at cold online leads hoping something will stick; thus, we have become much more profitable.

This financial and personal freedom has given me the opportunity to be a fully present and involved mother to my three children and a supportive wife to my husband, who also has a business of his own—and yes, he has used Magnetic Marketing principles to grow his business too, which has given our family even more freedom, and it's fun for us to compare and cross-pollinate ideas from his industry to mine, and back and forth. His business is www.HapiGig.com; it's like Uber for warehouse workers, and the owners of warehouses nationwide just love it!

Thanks to what we've both learned about how to manage a small law firm—and how to manage a small business, including Magnetic Marketing—we are able to enjoy extended international adventures with our family without having to worry about the day-to-day operation of the firm. The financial gain has not only helped provide an extraordinary life for my family and me, but it also has allowed me to hire an amazing team of superstars for each firm that make me feel tremendously fulfilled as a professional, and I love being able to employ a team that continually challenges me to keep learning and growing as a business owner and leader.

ABOUT RJON ROBINS

RJon Robins believes in profit, and he detests loss. And it's likely he knows more about how to start, manage, and grow a successful small law firm than anyone else alive today. Here's why …

At nine o'clock in the morning on August 24, 1999, RJon reported for duty as a Small Law Practice Management Advisor for The Florida Bar's Law Office Management Assistance Service (LOMAS)—he was there for four years and had the unique opportunity to work with nearly nine thousand separate solo or small law firm owners helping them tackle practically every law firm management, marketing, mindset, sales, staffing, cash flow, and profitability problem and opportunity imaginable.

RJon is the first, and to date the only, lawyer in the history of the Florida Bar to serve in this role. And Florida is one of only about a dozen states in the world that even have a Law Office Management Assistance program to help owners of law firms with the sort of practical, real-world law firm management challenges that any rational and intelligent person should anticipate would likely befall a person with only a law license but no prior marketing, sales, management, or financial controls experience when he or she decides to start a business that happens to be a law firm.

Those frontline experiences in the trenches—with thousands of law firms per year—influenced RJon's career, which has ever since been devoted to exposing and crushing The Doctrine of Sacrifice that infects the legal industry and teaches lawyers that sacrifice is not the means to the end but rather that sacrifice for the sake of sacrifice is the end. RJon says:

> When a person makes a conscious and intentional choice to sacrifice something he or she values less, as part of a rational plan to gain something of more value to him or herself, that's called making a profit. The pursuit of profit is what has raised up the human from the mean existence of the cave dweller to the life of abundance that is available to any person who would make use of the resources of modern society; by comparison, when a person makes a conscious or careless choice to sacrifice something he or she professes to value more and knows, or should know, the exchange will leave him or her only with something he or she values less, that's The Doctrine of Sacrifice in action—loss for the sake of loss. There's nothing noble about settling for loss as a way of life.

RJon believes that running a profitable business is among the highest callings of a human being.

That's what RJon believes. However, putting it all into practical action is a different matter altogether, and so after failing to follow his own (excellent) advice about building a systems-based business, when a severe unexpected illness suddenly afflicted RJon's wife, he ended up losing his home to foreclosure and found himself flat broke. After nursing his wife back to health in 2009, RJon picked himself up and began following his own (excellent) advice about not settling for less than a systems-based business.

Today, RJon is Cofounder and President of How To Manage Enterprises and one of its subsidiaries, How to Manage a Small Law Firm, which helps to manage more than four hundred of the fastest-growing, and some of the most profitable, solo and small law firms across the United States, in every practice area anyone could likely imagine, in cooperation with law firm owners from all walks of life.

How to Manage a Small Law Firm has been named by *Inc.* magazine as one of the five thousand fastest-growing privately held companies in the country six years in a row after having grown by more than TEN THOUSAND PERCENT since RJon started the business from his dining room table in 2009—which, if you've been following along, was the same year RJon lost his home to foreclosure and found himself "aspiring to be 'just broke.'" Oh yeah, and in case you forgot, in 2008 and 2009 there was a massive economic crash too.

"Our growth could not have happened had it not been for the success of the solo and small law firms we help to manage. And my most amazing team, whom I am so proud of and honored to work with," RJon is quick to add.

All of the portfolio companies owned and operated by How To Manage Enterprises share RJon's commitment to liberating entrepreneurial law firm owners from The Doctrine of Sacrifice by helping them build more successful businesses that support happier and more successful and more meaningful lives.

In addition to How to Manage a Small Law Firm, some of the portfolio companies include The Small Law Firm University; The Small Law Firm Owner's Unfair Advantage; The Small Law Firm Marketing Machine; The Show Them You Give A Shit Client Relationship Management Company; Small Law Firm Bookkeeping That Does Not Suck; Profitable Law Firm Marketing Videos That Actually Sell Legal Services!; and more.

RJon practices what he preaches about demanding that your business give you a life instead of the other way around. He is an avid boater and lives in South Florida with his wife and cofounder, Ale, their son, Taye Astuya, a dog, one or more cats, a flock of peacocks, and wild iguanas that live in their yard.

CPSIA information can be obtained
at www.ICGtesting.com
Printed in the USA
JSHW020341310321
13049JS00007B/247

9 781642 252651